Making Music with GarageBand® and Mixcraft™

Robin Hodson, James Frankel, Michael Fein, and Richard McCready

Course Technology PTR

A part of Cengage Learning

COURSE TECHNOLOGY
CENGAGE Learning™

Australia • Brazil • Japan • Korea • Mexico • Singapore • Spain • United Kingdom • United States

COURSE TECHNOLOGY
CENGAGE Learning

**Making Music with GarageBand®
and Mixcraft™
Robin Hodson, James Frankel,
Michael Fein, and Richard McCready**

Publisher and General Manager, Course Technology PTR: Stacy L. Hiquet

Associate Director of Marketing: Sarah Panella

Manager of Editorial Services: Heather Talbot

Marketing Manager: Mark Hughes

Executive Editor: Mark Garvey

Project Editor/Copy Editor: Cathleen D. Small

Interior Layout Tech: MPS Limited, a Macmillan Company

Cover Designer: Luke Fletcher

DVD-ROM Producer: Brandon Penticuff

Indexer: Sharon Shock

Proofreader: Gene Redding

About the Authors

Robin Hodson is the mid-Atlantic manager for SoundTree, based in Baltimore, Maryland. Robin comes from a musical family; his grandfather founded a symphony orchestra and music conservatory in Zimbabwe, and his mother taught music for 50 years. An accomplished composer and performer working in a variety of genres, he is also a recording engineer, songwriter, and arranger. Robin received a master's degree from Magdalen College, Oxford, before moving to the United States in 1999.

Dr. James Frankel is the managing director of SoundTree, the leader in music, audio, and video technology solutions for educators. Before taking the helm at SoundTree, he was the instrumental and general music teacher at Franklin Avenue Middle School in Franklin Lakes, New Jersey, for 11 years. Dr. Frankel earned a bachelor of music degree from Montclair State University and his master's and doctoral degrees in Music Education at Teachers College, Columbia University. An adjunct faculty member at Teachers College, Columbia University, he teaches a variety of courses on music technology. His published works include more than 50 articles in various state, national, and international journals of music education and several works published by SoundTree and Hal Leonard. Recently, his chapter entitled "Music Education Technology" was included in *Critical Issues in Music Education*, published by Oxford University Press. Dr. Frankel is on the board of directors for TI:ME, where he serves as the vice president/secretary and the editor of the TI:ME email newsletter. In addition to his work with the TI:ME national organization, he is the president of ATMI—the Association for Technology in Music Instruction.

Michael Fein earned a bachelor of music education degree from Rutgers University and a master's degree in jazz saxophone performance from Rowan University. Michael has published articles and lesson plans with *MET* magazine and SoundTree. He has presented numerous sessions at music and technology conferences, including the 2005 National Education Computing Conference in Philadelphia, Pennsylvania; the 2009 TI:ME National Conference in San Antonio, Texas; and the 2010 TI:ME National Conference in New Brunswick, New Jersey. Michael currently teaches music technology electives and the jazz ensemble at Haverford High School and serves as an adjunct jazz saxophone instructor at Swarthmore College. Michael's resume includes performances with Ralph Peterson, Stanley Cowell, Scott Whitfield, Ralph Bowen, Denis DiBlasio, Arden Theater Company, and lead alto work with the great Ray Charles. Michael released his debut CD entitled *Four Flights Up* in April 2005. The CD features Michael and his jazz sextet performing original tunes and arrangements. The CD was re-released by Dreambox Media in October 2006 and is now available for purchase through Amazon.com, DreamboxMedia.com, and select local record stores.

Richard McCready teaches music technology at River Hill High School in Howard County, Maryland. He also serves the Howard County school district in a resource capacity, training other teachers and helping them to bring the excitement of music technology to their students. Richard earned his bachelor's degree from the Royal Northern College of Music in Manchester, England, and his master's degrees from Towson University in Towson, Maryland. Richard has been teaching for 20 years and has taught at the middle school, high school, and college levels. Throughout Richard's career, he has taught students to experience music through creativity and composition, always using the latest wave of available technology, from 4-track cassette-tape recorders to modern-day DAWs, such as Pro Tools, Ableton Live, GarageBand, and Acoustica Mixcraft.

Contents

Chapter 4
Getting Started with Mixcraft   59

Chapter 5
Getting Started with GarageBand   69

Chapter 6
Getting Started with MIDI in Mixcraft   81

Chapter 7
Getting Started with MIDI in GarageBand   93

Chapter 8
Recording Your Own Audio in Mixcraft   109

Chapter 9
Recording Your Own Audio in GarageBand   119

Chapter 10
Creating Podcasts in Mixcraft   133

Chapter 11
Creating Podcasts in GarageBand   143

Chapter 12
Working with Video in Mixcraft   157

Chapter 16
Putting It All Together: Two Final Projects for Mixcraft or GarageBand — 219

Chapter 17
Putting It All Together — 229

DVD-ROM Downloads

If you purchased an ebook version of this book, and the book had a companion DVD-ROM, you may download the contents from www.courseptr.com/downloads.

If your book has a DVD-ROM, please check our website for any updates or errata files. You may download files from www.courseptr.com/downloads.

1 | Introduction

Teaching creativity in the music classroom has always been something of an enigma in the traditional school music program. For whatever reason, many music teachers find it difficult to teach their students how to be creative—specifically through music composition. One reason may be that so few university music education programs require their pre-service music educators (those who have yet to start teaching) to create an original composition as part of their graduation requirements. Another reason might be that music education programs focus on performance rather than creativity. It may be that teachers believe creativity can't actually be taught; it can only be nurtured.

Perhaps one of the practical roadblocks for fostering creativity in the music classroom is that it takes time and money. Between allowing students time to work on their projects (either individually or in groups), providing constructive feedback, and showcasing student work, a teacher needs to make a firm commitment to give students the freedom to be creative in their classrooms. Maybe teachers feel that the costs of the tools necessary for students to compose are quite high—especially if that teacher believes it takes a state-of-the-art music technology lab to get students composing.

Additionally, understanding those tools enough to teach them is a challenge for many music educators. Effective and ongoing professional development is a crucial factor in successfully implementing a creativity-focused unit or curriculum. Or perhaps the real reason is that in order to truly foster a creative, nurturing environment in the music classroom, educators need to take a more collaborative approach to teaching. Rather than being the sage on the stage, a teacher must transform into the guide on the side. Instead of assessing student work as right or wrong, teachers have to take a draft/edit/revise, qualitative approach to assessment.

Whatever the reason, this resistance to fostering creativity in the music classroom is real, and it must end.

Fortunately, there are some incredible music programs taught by outstanding music educators around the United States and the world that can serve as models for fostering a creative, nurturing environment in K-12 music classrooms. What many of these programs have in common is an energetic and passionate music educator, a supportive administration, fantastic students, and some common tools. What students produce

1

in these programs is nothing short of remarkable. The following story reflects the impact of these programs and the amazing work that their students produce.

Note: A well-known composer for cable television documentaries recently lamented the dwindling opportunities for work due to increasing competition from high school and college students who were producing high-quality, self-produced, loop-based compositions on their laptops using software and hardware that cost less than $200. During the conversation, he reflected on the recent past, where the only way to produce 60 minutes' worth of music for a television program was to utilize expensive hardware and software to actually compose the music and then hire a live orchestra to record the music in a state-of-the-art recording studio. Whereas once he would get $50,000 or more for a one-hour program, now the going rate is $2,000. He blames inexpensive software and hardware that make it easy for anyone to compose for this dramatic change, as well as an army of really creative kids who do amazing things with music. On one hand he is excited by the notion of the flattening of the creative world, and on the other hand, he misses those paychecks.

This story helps to illustrate the power of the tools our students have at their disposal, the creative opportunities that those tools facilitate, and most importantly, the incredible potential in all of the students we teach. Most music production software titles available today cost less than $300. Quite a few of those are less than $100, and some are free. The tools included in these programs are powerful enough to create a product worthy of inclusion in professional productions. Many of the programs include copyright- and royalty-free loops (short snippets of audio containing musical phrases or motives) that allow nontraditional (and traditional) music students to compose music without having to know how to read music. Most importantly, learning these programs takes relatively little time, and the students that we teach are often extremely comfortable using them before we even introduce the program in our classroom.

It is clear that the students in our classrooms today want to create content in the same medium in which they consume it. Mixcraft and GarageBand allow students to do just that. This book is meant to provide music educators with a comprehensive guide to these two specific software titles, Mixcraft and GarageBand, with a focus on how you can use the software to allow students opportunities to be creative. It includes:

- A pedagogical rationale for using sequencing/music production software in the music classroom

- In-depth tutorials on how to use each of the software programs

- Conceptually based lesson plans written by two outstanding music educators whose programs serve as models for creativity and nurturing classroom environments

- Recommendations for peripheral hardware and software that will enhance the functionality of the software

- Ideas for extending each lesson plan

- Best-practice examples

- A companion website with additional resources

It is the authors' sincere hope that this book provides music educators with a roadmap for using these two incredible programs with their students to foster musical creativity—whether you are a teacher just starting out with technology or you are experienced with music technology and are looking for additional teaching resources to use with your students.

Why Sequencing Software?

Music educators have only a few basic software choices when it comes to music composition: notation software and sequencing software. Although there are some other specific software titles out there that may not fit these two categories exactly, the vast majority of them do.

Notation software was initially created as a tool for professional music copyists and has since become one of the main tools for educators looking to incorporate composition into their curriculum. Many educators consider notation software the more traditional approach to music composition, where students need to be able to notate and read their musical ideas in order to be successful at composition. Programs such as Finale and Sibelius include tools that help students capture their musical ideas on paper and allow them to choose whether their final product is meant to be played back using realistic-sounding virtual instruments or by printing out their finished composition and having live performers re-create their work.

This approach to teaching composition is certainly valid and worthwhile, but it does have a specific drawback. Many—if not the majority—of the students in our classrooms do not read music at all, and they may feel unprepared or inadequate when completing composition assignments using notation software.

Music sequencing software provides an alternative to notation-based composition. The term *sequencer* literally means creating a sequence of musical events over time. Those musical events can include pitches, rests, note durations, dynamics, fragments of audio, tempo, time signature, changes in velocity, timbres, and video clips.

Early sequencers could only create short musical patterns consisting of one note at a time. Since then, sequencers have advanced to the point where they are more commonly known as *digital audio workstations* or *music production software*. Sequencers can now sequence almost anything over time, including recorded audio, video, loops, MIDI files, virtual instruments, and more.

Whereas notation programs are primarily meant to document and print musical ideas for live performances, sequencing programs are meant to capture musical ideas and events for playback on a computer or media player. Another strong distinction between notation and sequencing software is that sequencing software does not require knowledge of music notation to produce a successful project. While most sequencing software includes an optional notation window, the primary way to capture musical thoughts is through performance. From a pedagogical standpoint, it could be argued that:

Notation software = traditional music student

Sequencing software = nontraditional music student

This distinction makes a very compelling argument when teachers consider how to foster creative opportunities for the greatest number of students. While traditional music students can be successful no matter which type of software they use, nontraditional music students can be successful only when using sequencers (though there can certainly be exceptions to this rule) because it is not necessary to be able to read music. It is up to the individual teacher, of course, to choose which road to take, but it is important to consider how to engage the nontraditional music student when using only notation software for composition.

Why Mixcraft?

Mixcraft is a software program that was created by a company called Acoustica. Founded in 2002, its motto is "Software should be easy to use." Currently in version 5, Mixcraft is an affordable, feature-packed, easy-to-use digital audio workstation. The software interface is very user friendly and is set up in the traditional multitrack recorder orientation (see Figure 1.1). The controls are easy to locate and understand, and students will have little difficulty learning how to get started.

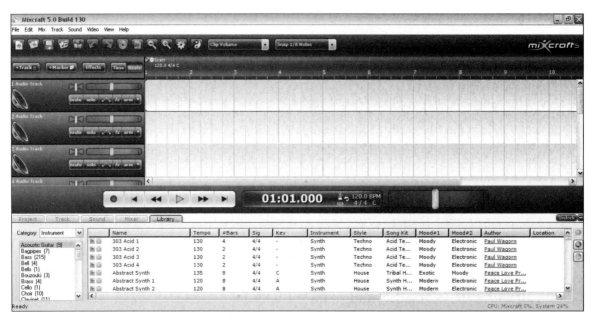

Figure 1.1 Mixcraft interface.

Current features include:

- Unlimited audio and MIDI tracks

- More than 3,000 copyright- and royalty-free loops

- Large collection of virtual instruments

- Video integration

- Notation tools

- Effects processors, including guitar amplifier simulators

- Ability to import .mid, .mp3, .ogg, .wav, .aiff, and .wma files

- Ability to export recordings as .mp3, .ogg, .wav, and .wma files or directly to CD

Note: Note that as of this printing, Mixcraft will run only on Windows-based operating systems.

Tip: For a full list of the features of Mixcraft, visit www.acoustica.com/mixcraft.

Mixcraft is an intuitive program. When you first launch the software, it prompts you to select from three options: Record Yourself or Your Band, Build Loop & Beat Matched Music, or Build Virtual Instrument Tracks (see Figure 1.2). These three options allow you to capture and create quite a large variety of musical compositions—everything from live recordings, to remixes and mash-ups, to loop-based compositions.

Figure 1.2 Mixcraft New Project window.

The reason that we selected Mixcraft over the many other similar programs that are available is because, in our opinion, it is the closest match to the features and functionality of GarageBand, and the lessons contained in this book are easily transferable to either program. As you will read in a moment, when comparing the two software titles, Mixcraft and GarageBand are very similar. Additionally, we have selected Mixcraft as the single most easy-to-use PC-based software sequencer, with a tremendous variety of uses within the music curriculum. A detailed tutorial on Mixcraft follows in Chapter 2, "Getting Started with Mixcraft."

Why GarageBand?

Apple first introduced GarageBand in 2004 as a part of the iLife Suite—a collection of creative productivity applications that come standard with the purchase of any Apple computer, specifically the Macintosh line of laptop and desktop computers. Currently in its sixth version (named GarageBand '11), GarageBand is a very popular and easy-to-use music software program. The GarageBand interface is very clean, and like Mixcraft, the controls are easy to understand and use (see Figure 1.3). Like Mixcraft, GarageBand employs a drag-and-drop interface in which users simply click on media or content that they would like to use or edit and drag it to the appropriate location.

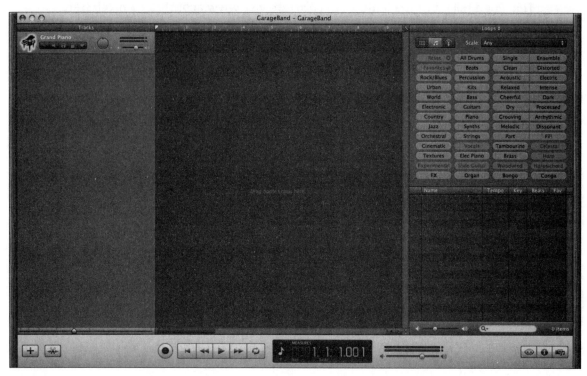

Figure 1.3 GarageBand interface.

Current features include:

- Ability to record up to 255 Real Instrument tracks (depending on CPU).

- Ability to record up to 64 Software Instrument tracks.

- Thousands of copyright- and royalty-free loops.

- Five additional JamPacks with thousands of loops, virtual instruments, and effects.

- More than 100 virtual instruments.

- Video and podcasting integration.

- Notation tool.

- Effects processors, including guitar amplifier simulators.

- Ability to import .mid, .aiff, .wav, and .mp3 files.

- Ability to export audio recordings as .aiff or directly to CD. Videos are exported as .mov files.

Note: As of this printing, GarageBand will run only on Apple computers.

Tip: For a full list of the features of GarageBand, visit www.apple.com/ilife/garageband.

GarageBand is also a very intuitive program. As GarageBand was released before Mixcraft, some would argue that the easy-to-use interface seen in Mixcraft is largely based on the features of GarageBand—specifically, the drag-and-drop interface, the library of loops, and the easy-to-understand controls. Either way, both programs are perfect entry-level sequencers packed with powerful features.

When you first open GarageBand, it prompts you to select what type of project you would like to begin (see Figure 1.4). Rather than the three options for Mixcraft, GarageBand offers quite a few more, including:

- **New Project.** Here you can create your own music composition, film score, or podcast. Options include Piano, Electric Guitar, Voice, Loops, Keyboard Collection, Acoustic Instrument, Songwriting, and Podcast.

- **Learn to Play.** Here you can watch videos containing lessons on piano and guitar.

- **Lesson Store.** Here you can purchase lessons taught by celebrity musicians.

- **Magic GarageBand.** Here you can set up a backing track in a variety of styles.

- **iPhone Ringtone.** Here you can create your own iPhone ringtones.

The reason why many teachers who use Macs in their classrooms find GarageBand so useful is that it can serve so many different functions—from recording performances, to podcasting, to film scoring, to facilitating composition in the classroom. (Mixcraft also serves these same functions.)

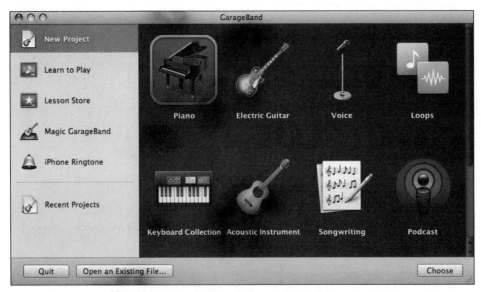

Figure 1.4 GarageBand New Project window.

Although there are quite a few other Mac-based sequencing programs available, none matches all of this set of features while also being free with every Mac. There are certainly some drawbacks in terms of features that are missing in GarageBand (there are no time signature changes, and you can't export as MIDI or reverse recordings), they are somewhat insignificant when compared to what GarageBand *can* do. A detailed tutorial on GarageBand follows in Chapter 3, "Getting Started with GarageBand."

Pedagogical Considerations

So how can you use Mixcraft and GarageBand in your classroom? What grade levels are appropriate? Can band and chorus directors use Mixcraft and GarageBand? What do you need to get started? All of these questions are important to ask and answer before you go any further with this book. Here are the answers:

■ Performance-based classes can simply use Mixcraft or GarageBand as a way to capture live performances and to publish those performances to media such as compact discs or downloadable audio files. Teachers can also post those recordings to facilitate critical-reflection activities.

■ General music classrooms can use Mixcraft or GarageBand as a way to facilitate composition activities, including:

   ■ Composing within specified guidelines

   ■ Creating loop-based compositions

   ■ Understanding basic audio-engineering concepts

   ■ Working on film scoring

   ■ Podcasting

- Teachers can use Mixcraft or GarageBand to create instructional materials for their students.

- Students can use Mixcraft or GarageBand in school or at home to explore creative music-making and music-capturing opportunities.

For the purposes of this book, the lesson plans are geared toward middle school and high school students. That does not mean you can't use either program with students in grades K–5. There are some terrific publications and web resources available that include lesson ideas for those grade levels, specifically *Technology Integration in the Elementary Music Classroom* (Hal Leonard, 2008) by Amy M. Burns. As a tool for creating educational materials and recordings for your students, any music teacher can use both programs.

In terms of what you need to get started using Mixcraft and GarageBand, you must first look at the classroom environment in which you teach and what departmental budgets will allow. Although there is little question that the optimal teaching environment for incorporating sequencing software is a state-of-the-art music technology lab including computers, keyboards, software, networking, and furniture, this might not always be possible. We have included several scenarios in the following sections that describe various teaching situations and contain suggestions for how you might incorporate sequencing software in those specific situations.

Classroom Environments

Music educators are often faced with a number of different teaching environments. For those lucky enough to have their own classrooms, the following sections address the various ways in which technology can be implemented into the classroom environment. For those music educators who do not have their own classrooms, it is difficult, though not impossible, to utilize technology with your students. You can use Mixcraft and GarageBand both as a way to create materials for your students and as a way to record student performances.

The One-Computer Classroom

More often than not, music teachers have only one computer to use with their students in a classroom. Sometimes the computer is their own personal computer, as there is no budget to purchase one for the music department. In this scenario there are specific challenges that create some issues for successful implementation of sequencing software, including the following.

- Only one student (or teacher) will be able to compose at a time.

- The students will need to see the computer screen.

- The students will need to hear the products created using the software.

You must address each of these challenges before using Mixcraft or GarageBand with your students. Unfortunately, there is no free solution that collectively will solve each of these problems. The first challenge (one student/teacher composing at a time) will always remain, unfortunately, but it should not serve as a deterrent to using the software.

First, you can use Mixcraft and GarageBand solely to create teaching materials—including podcasts, listening guides, listening examples, accompaniment recordings, and so on. Second, you can use Mixcraft or GarageBand to provide enrichment activities for individual students. To use it with the students in a class setting, though, you'll need to be a bit creative with the types of activities you will do with your students. Ideas for whole-class integration in a one-computer classroom include teaching the basics of sound and acoustics, creating a class song, teaching the techniques of film scoring, recording podcasts, and creating listening examples.

To effectively use sequencing software with an entire class in a one-computer setting, it is vital to include some type of projection device and sound amplification. If you have access to an LCD projector, you will need to project your computer onto a screen so that all of your students can see what you're doing. It's always best to have a permanently mounted LCD projector in your classroom, but if that is not available, a portable LCD projector on a cart will suffice.

The best situation, however, would be to have some brand of digital interactive whiteboard in your classroom. Interactive whiteboards allow students to come up to the board and use their fingers to interact with the software. Both Mixcraft and GarageBand work very well with any brand of interactive whiteboard. If you don't have access to either an LCD projector or an interactive whiteboard, you might consider bringing your class down to the school computer lab (described in a moment).

When students don't have the ability to see what you're doing, classroom management will be exceptionally challenging. In addition to the visual aspect, it is important to have some type of amplification for your computer. You can achieve this through a set of computer audio speakers, an amplifier, or an integrated sound system that includes your computer audio. You will most likely need an adapter and/or an audio cable to connect your computer to each of these options.

The School Computer Lab

If your school has a computer lab, and you're able to bring your students to it during your scheduled music class (either once a week or at a specific block of time), your students can get far more hands-on experience with music making using Mixcraft or GarageBand. If your school is Mac-based, you already have GarageBand loaded on the machines. If your school is PC-based, purchasing a site license for Mixcraft is very affordable, and you can request that your IT department purchase it for the lab, rather than using your own departmental budget.

To effectively use Mixcraft or GarageBand in your school computer lab, you should consider purchasing two basic peripheral devices: headphones and an inexpensive USB keyboard controller. Additionally, an interactive whiteboard is quite useful for demonstrating software functions, and software programs such as Apple Remote Desktop and Vision are great for monitoring student activity while in the computer lab.

The Music Technology Lab

As stated earlier, the best solution for incorporating Mixcraft or GarageBand into your music curriculum is a stand-alone music technology lab. By definition, a music technology lab consists of multiple student stations, each containing a computer with a variety of music software titles, a keyboard (either piano or synthesizer with MIDI connectivity or a USB keyboard controller), a digital audio interface device, and headphones. Some type of lab controller and networking hardware makes the lab much easier to teach in. Both Mixcraft and GarageBand are ideally suited for integration into a music technology lab. Benefits of this type of classroom environment include the following:

- Each student can work independently or in pairs, allowing for more hands-on experience and time spent creating and composing.

- There are no scheduling issues when planning a composition unit, as there will be when dealing with a school computer lab.

- The computers are set up to be used only by your students, rather than having many other software titles (which may cause conflicts) loaded, as in a school computer lab.

- Students get valuable experience using industry-standard tools and develop 21st-century learning skills.

> **Tip:** The lesson plans contained in this publication are best suited for lab environments, using either a school computer lab or a music technology lab. Although it is certainly possible to adapt some of the lessons for a one-computer classroom, it is not the ideal teaching situation.

To Loop or Not to Loop?

That question is often raised when discussing the two software titles featured in this book, Mixcraft and GarageBand. Both programs contain what are known as *loops*—short segments of audio that students can drag into their compositions. The concept of looping has been around for quite some time, and music genres such as hip-hop and rap employ loops as the building blocks for creating songs. Many television shows, commercials, and film scores today use loops from both Mixcraft and GarageBand in their soundtracks. This may be one of the reasons why the composer in the story earlier in this chapter is losing work to younger composers who are willing to take less money—it takes less time to produce. Because both programs employ loops as one of the main ways to compose, it is important to look at the issue from an educational standpoint.

There are a number of ways to look at loops, and educators often struggle with how best to use them. On one hand, it takes very little musical knowledge to create compositions using loops. On the other hand, loops allow anyone to compose and feel good about what they create. Using loops is similar to creating a collage. You can add them to your work, play around with the positioning, and then add some more layers of loops until you have a finished product.

Opponents of loop-based composition see this process as using someone else's material—not creating anything truly original. Proponents of loop-based composition see using loops as a starting point for inspiring creativity. It is ultimately up to the individual teacher to decide when and how loops are used, but here are a few ideas to consider:

- Allow students to use loops extensively when they first start composing. It will hook them into the creative process.

- Gradually restrict students' use of loops as they become more and more confident and musically knowledgeable. For example, allow them to use only drum loops and bass loops when you want them to compose their own melody.

- Students will eventually tire of the included loops. This is a good thing. It will create a desire to know how to create new, original material.

- As a project idea, have the students create their own loops and add them to the loop library for others to use.

Looping is not the only thing you can do with Mixcraft and GarageBand, but it is certainly one of the most exciting things for students.

Other Software Titles

Obviously, there are many different sequencers available to musicians and educators, including Pro Tools, Logic, Digital Performer, Ableton Live, Reason, Record, SONAR, Cubase, Sony ACID, Cakewalk, and more. You can use the lessons and ideas contained within this book in any of these titles as long as you make some minor adaptations (for software-specific functions, video integration, and so on). You can teach a good lesson using any software program. It is our sincere hope that the lessons contained in this book fall into that category.

Obsolescence?

When writing any text on specific software titles, you naturally run the risk of having the text quickly become obsolete. We have written the lessons in this book based on broad musical concepts, which will hopefully protect them from a quick death. These concepts include:

- Getting started with existing audio

- Getting started with MIDI

- Recording your own audio

- Podcasting

- Working with film

- Multitrack recording, mixing, and mastering

- Putting it all together: MIDI/audio/video

Format of the Book and Lessons

Following this introductory chapter are two in-depth tutorials on how to use both Mixcraft and GarageBand. These tutorials include step-by-step instructions, illustrations, peripheral suggestions, and links to relevant related resources. After the tutorial section comes the heart of the book: a set of lesson plans written for Mixcraft and Garage-Band, categorized by larger concepts (as mentioned a moment ago). These lessons were written by two of the best music technology teachers in the country, Michael Fein and Richard McCready. Both have extensive experience with using these software titles with their students and will share best practices and tips on how to best integrate Mixcraft and GarageBand into your middle school and high school music curriculum.

2 Getting Started with Mixcraft: Skills Acquisition

This chapter will help you get familiar with the settings, screens, and buttons in Mixcraft and enable you to acquire skills that will be applied in the lessons accompanying this chapter.

There is a video on the disc accompanying these materials that follows these same steps, if you prefer to watch rather than read.

With any of these steps and materials, you can use the trial version of Mixcraft (downloadable from the www.acoustica.com/mixcraft website), but sooner or later you'll need to purchase a copy, as the trial version is time limited.

Opening a Song

Start by launching the software, and the floating window shown in Figure 2.1 will appear.

There are three choices of song that you can start with. For the moment, however, look toward the bottom of the window, where it says Load a Previous Project or Template, and choose Blood Pressurize.mx5, which is a sample song that comes with Mixcraft.

The screen should look like what you see in Figure 2.2.

The Preferences Box

Before you play or edit the song, now is a good time to familiarize yourself with the settings inside Mixcraft. Go to File > Preferences, and the dialog box shown in Figure 2.3 will appear.

Notice the 10 choices down the left-hand side, starting with Sound Device.

This first screen is where you can select your audio playback device, if you have an audio interface connected to your computer. It may also display your latency in milliseconds on that same screen. Latency is the amount of time the computer takes to process data (such as a digital audio wave or the pressing of a note on a MIDI keyboard) and translate that into sound you can hear. You want latency to be as low as possible. This is critical if you start recording with a connected device. If the latency is high (above 50 milliseconds), you might want to investigate downloading ASIO and using

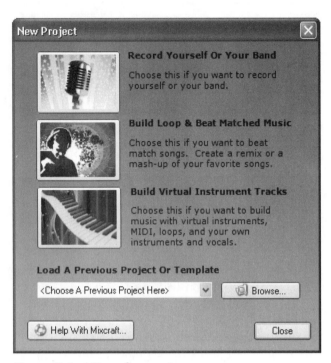

Figure 2.1 Mixcraft opening screen.

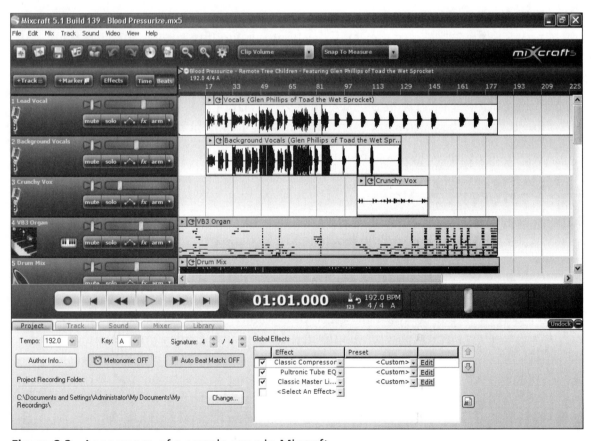

Figure 2.2 Appearance of a sample song in Mixcraft.

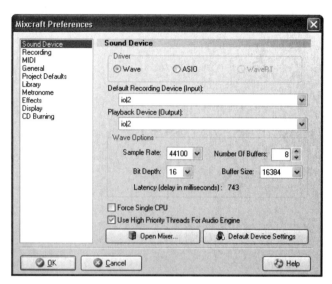

Figure 2.3 The Preferences dialog.

this as your driver for the software. Once again, consult your dealer's technical support department for more information. ASIO generally is the best choice for an audio driver on any Windows computer. It is free to download (from www.asio4all.com), and it lowers your latency.

Take a look through the settings on the other nine mini-screens. You shouldn't generally need to alter any of these choices. Click OK to quit the Preferences.

Testing Playback

Now you might want to test that playback is working on your computer. Locate the main playback controls on the screen, as shown in Figure 2.4.

Figure 2.4 Mixcraft's main playback controls.

These include all the standard controls, including Record, Fast Forward, Rewind to Beginning, and so forth. Click on the main Play button (or tap on the spacebar of your computer) to start and stop playback.

To play the song from a specific point, you can click on the timeline across the top of the screen, as shown in Figure 2.5.

You'll see a green flag appear as you click. Just choose a point and tap the spacebar or press Play.

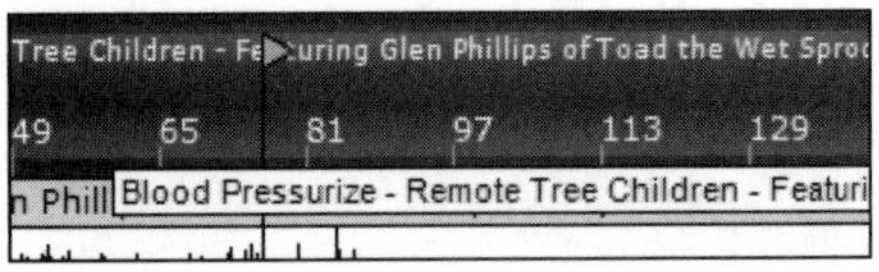

Figure 2.5 Clicking on the timeline of your project.

Understanding Track Settings

Notice the volume controls on each track on the left-hand side, as shown in Figure 2.6. Altering these will allow you to change the relative balance between tracks.

Figure 2.6 Panning and volume controls for each track.

Also locate the Solo and Mute buttons for each track and experiment with them.

One general point worth knowing (which is true for almost all software): If you hover your mouse over any button without clicking, the software will usually tell you what the button does.

You may wish to investigate what the other buttons on each track are for (see Figure 2.7). These will be covered in detail in later chapters.

Figure 2.7 The six buttons that appear on each Audio or MIDI track.

The Automation button (which looks like a small line graph) is very useful for making volume, panning, and effects changes to a track while it plays, but you can ignore it for now if you're a beginner to Mixcraft. The same applies to the FX button. The Arm button is only used if you're about to record straight into a track, so always ensure that this is turned off by default.

Also notice the icons to the far left of each track. These help denote what kind of track each one is (see Figure 2.8).

Tracks 1, 2, and 3 are clearly Audio tracks (with voices recorded), but Track 4 is different. There's a keyboard icon to indicate that it's a MIDI or Virtual Instrument track, and if you look closely, you'll see that the musical content inside the track is different as well—it's actually a series of MIDI events rather than digital sound waves. Click on the keyboard icon you see by the track name, and you can see all the possible choices of instrument you have in Mixcraft (see Figure 2.9).

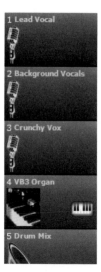

Figure 2.8 Icons below each track name.

Figure 2.9 Dialog box for changing the MIDI/virtual instrument.

Be careful here: If you click inside this box to alter the organ sound, it will change the sound of that track in your song, especially if you choose a different kind of instrument entirely. You may wish to close this box without making any changes at this time—but this is where you would alter sounds of MIDI tracks in the future.

Navigating and Zooming

On the right-hand side of the screen you'll see a vertical scroll bar, which allows you to see all the tracks in the song (in this case, 16). See Figure 2.10.

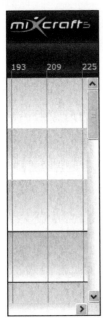

Figure 2.10 Vertical scroll bar on the far right.

Scroll up and down to see all the different tracks in the project.

Notice also the horizontal scroll bar (above the main green song counter/timer), which allows you to advance through the song to the end if you can't see all of the song on one screen.

Zooming in and out of the song is also worth learning at this stage. Locate the two zoom icons at the top of the screen, as shown in Figure 2.11.

Figure 2.11 The zoom icons in Mixcraft.

You may want to learn the shortcuts for zooming, which make the process faster—just use the minus and plus buttons on your computer keyboard. (You can use either the +/– buttons on the main QWERTY keyboard (with or without Shift) or the +/– buttons on the numeric keypad on the right-hand side of the QWERTY keyboard.) If you have a scroll wheel on your mouse, you can also use this for zooming. Try these out to get familiar with them.

Another good setting to learn at this early stage is whether to display your song in time or beats. Locate the buttons toward the top of the screen, as shown in Figure 2.12.

Figure 2.12 Mixcraft icons for changing your timeline/counter display.

See what happens when you choose Time instead of Beats. Your choice will depend a lot on what kind of song you're working with. If you do a project that requires playing in notes from a MIDI keyboard, you'll probably want your song in beats. For recording sounds that do not depend on beat matching, such as voiceover, speech, podcasts, and film composing (see later chapters), you'll probably want to set the display to Time.

Basic Editing and Understanding How Regions Work

Any Mixcraft song (project) is made up of *tracks*, and each track has *regions* (or *clips*) within it. Try to remember that terminology, as it comes up often when you're working with the software. You can move any region in the song by picking it up by its header (where you see the name of the individual region) and dragging it with your mouse to the left or right. Try it with the first region that you see in Track 1 of the song, as shown in Figure 2.13.

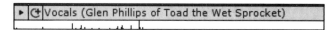

Figure 2.13   The header of a region in Mixcraft.

Notice also that if you click on the tiny loop icon that is across the top of each snippet of music (see Figure 2.14), you'll get another copy of that same region. It is created in the next available space on the timeline, and you can drag this new region around independently. Using this technique, you'll see that you can quickly extend the format of your song.

Figure 2.14   The Loop button on any region in Mixcraft.

Now hover your mouse over any of the regions in the first three tracks, and you'll see that the mouse cursor alters between being a standard I-beam cursor (for selecting a point in the audio) and being a crosshair-style cursor (for making a change to the volume of a track). Be careful when your cursor changes to a crosshair—for the moment you want it to be the I-beam cursor, so you can do some editing of a region. Select somewhere in the middle of a region, and you'll notice a dotted line appears below, as shown in Figure 2.15.

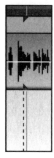

Figure 2.15   Dotted line when a selection is made.

You can now split the region at this point, using the shortcut Ctrl+T (or by choosing Edit > Split). Your region will now be chopped into two regions or clips, and you can move each region/clip independently or delete one. To delete any region/clip entirely, select it and press the Backspace or Delete key.

You can use this technique for any Audio or MIDI tracks in your song. Cut any audio or MIDI region in any track, create extra copies of it (using the techniques mentioned earlier), and drag the regions around on the timeline.

You can also drag a region from one track to another, but be careful when you do this. Generally, you'll want to keep musical material within the same track. Also, you can't drag an audio region into a MIDI track and vice versa.

The Details Section

At the lower part of the screen, you'll see the Details section. It should currently look like what you see in Figure 2.16.

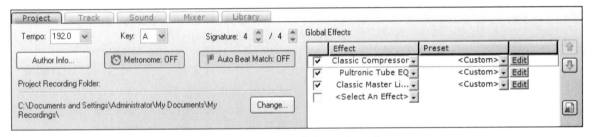

Figure 2.16 The Details section at the bottom of the Mixcraft screen.

It will currently be set to the Project tab, which gives the main information about the song (tempo, key, and time signature). You can alter these (and doing so will affect the song), so be careful about the choices you make!

Mixcraft is clever at making changes to both Audio and MIDI tracks if you alter the tempo of a song, but think about this musically. If someone has sung a vocal at a specific tempo, it's going to be somewhat disruptive to change the speed of what the person already recorded! Software has become adept at coping with this, but it's not an ideal state of affairs—the audio region will definitely start to degrade when you alter its tempo. Generally speaking, try not to alter the tempo of a project once you've started working on it, for musical safety's sake and for the quality of the sounds you record.

The same largely applies to altering the key and the time signature of a song as well. It's just not something you should do without thinking through the consequences!

The Project tab also shows you what effects you're using in the song as a whole. Once again, for the moment you probably won't want to alter these. Bear in mind that each track may have individual effects that it uses, and you're more likely to make alterations to the individual track than to make them on this screen.

Take a look at a few of the other tabs. The Track tab allows you to customize the color of each of your tracks, and it shows what effects you might be using (see Figure 2.17).

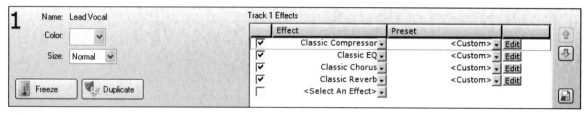

Figure 2.17 The Track tab at the bottom of the screen.

With this tab displayed, click on any track in the song (near the name of the track, on the left), and you'll see all the different information for each track. Changing the color is sometimes helpful to assist you when you're working with many tracks in a song.

You'll notice that the Track tab also has Freeze and Duplicate buttons, which are useful at times. There are moments when you might want to lock a track so that it cannot be edited or changed too much. There are also times when you may wish to make an entirely new copy of a track. You may not need these features yet. If you do try one of these features, you can usually undo any action you take by typing Ctrl+Z (the universal shortcut used by Windows computer programs to undo an action).

The Track tab will once again display the effects currently in use. Again, you probably wouldn't change the effects in use on this actual screen.

The Sound tab behaves a little differently, depending on whether you're working with an Audio track or a MIDI track. With this tab chosen, click on any region you see on the track timeline. (Click on the header at the top of each region; see Figure 2.18.)

Figure 2.18 The header of one of the regions in your project.

If you click on any of the regions in Track 4 or 7, you'll see the notes displayed in either Piano Roll view or Notation view. (You can toggle between these views using two buttons toward the bottom of the Sound tab—one looks like a series of horizontal bars, and the other looks like a music note.) The Sound tab should look like what you see in Figure 2.19.

You'll notice a whole new set of tools has appeared just above where you see the notation. You can edit MIDI data by clicking on notes, moving them up and down, and adding extra notes. All of this will be covered in more detail in later chapters.

Now if you look back up the screen to see some of the other regions in your song, locate one that looks like an audio region instead. (You may need to use the vertical scroll bar on the far right of the screen to get to other regions/tracks in the song.) Click

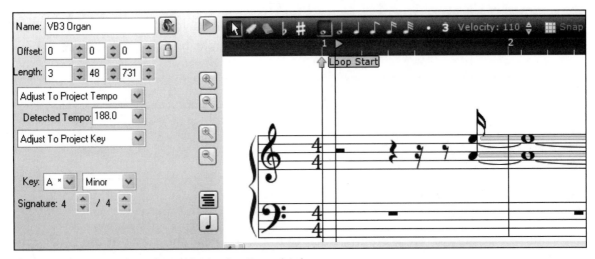

Figure 2.19   Notation view within the Sound tab.

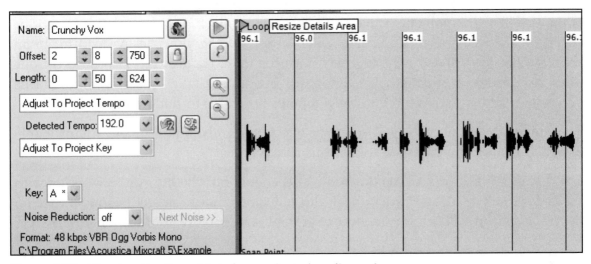

Figure 2.20   Viewing the Sound tab for a selected audio region.

on an audio region. Remember to click on the header of a region, exactly where it is named. You should now see what is shown in Figure 2.20 in the Sound window down below.

You'll see the audio region you selected, and this is where you can do detailed editing. Once again, we'll leave this skill for later chapters.

One final detail worth knowing: If you ever want to switch to the Sound window when you're working in Mixcraft, just double-click on the header at the top of a region (where it is named). Mixcraft will automatically guess that you want to work on the Sound window rather than any of the other tabs.

The Mixer tab is pretty self-explanatory. It's simply a horizontal view of all the channel strips of your tracks, including volume, panning, solo/mute, FX, EQ, and sends (see

Figure 2.21). This is often easier than using the volume and pan sliders on each track (farther up the screen).

Figure 2.21 The Mixer tab at the bottom of the Mixcraft screen.

Note, though, that on the left-hand side you can restrict which faders you want to look at by clicking on Audio, Virtual Instrument (the MIDI tracks), and Send, as shown in Figure 2.22. (Send tracks are rather more advanced and will be covered in later chapters.)

Figure 2.22 Types of tracks that can be displayed in the Mixer.

Let's go over the Mixer tab in some more detail. Each channel strip looks like a channel strip on a hardware mixer—the type you would see in a recording studio. The big vertical sliders control volume level, with a digital readout beside each of the sliders showing how loud the output of each track is. You'll also see EQ buttons above each fader. EQ is a critical part of learning to mix in a real studio, and it is every bit as important as setting good volume levels, choosing the right effects, and panning a song left to right in the stereo spectrum. Soloing a track in your song and then playing with the EQ, you'll notice how big a difference it can make. You'll also see that there's an FX button for choosing whether your track has effects on it, plus Mute and Solo buttons (M and S, respectively, below the EQ knobs). Just below that you'll see the panning slider, which will allow you to move your sound left or right in the mix. There's plenty to play with in the Mixer tab.

The final tab, which says Library, is strictly for when you want to build your own song using loops (preexisting musical material). See Figure 2.23.

Category: Tempo		Name	Tem...	#Bars	Sig	Key	Instrum...	Style	Song...	Mood...	Mood...	Author	L
050 - 059 (10)		Advance Tone 1				-	Sound E...	Navi...	Soun...	Podc...	Radio	freesfx.co...	
060 - 069 (1)		Advance Tone 10				-	Sound E...	Navi...	Soun...	Podc...	Radio	freesfx.co...	
070 - 079 (8)		Advance Tone 11				-	Sound E...	Navi...	Soun...	Podc...	Radio	freesfx.co...	
080 - 089 (224)		Advance Tone 12				-	Sound E...	Navi...	Soun...	Podc...	Radio	freesfx.co...	
090 - 099 (226)		Advance Tone 13				-	Sound E...	Navi...	Soun...	Podc...	Radio	freesfx.co...	C
100 - 109 (190)		Advance Tone 14				-	Sound E...	Navi...	Soun...	Podc...	Radio	freesfx.co...	
110 - 119 (368)		Advance Tone 15				-	Sound E...	Navi...	Soun...	Podc...	Radio	freesfx.co...	
120 - 129 (297)													

Figure 2.23 The Library tab at the bottom of the screen.

You'll be using these loops in a short while when you build a song. There's a huge amount of musical material available to use. If you want to audition any loop before dragging it into your song, you can click on the blue Play icon next to each loop. Don't click on the green plus button, though—this will add the loop into your song wherever your cursor was last positioned. See Figure 2.24.

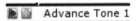

Figure 2.24 The Audition button for any loop.

On the left-hand side of the Library tab, you'll see that you can select or filter your loops by a variety of parameters. There are many categories to choose from, as you can see in Figure 2.25.

Category: Tempo

Tempo
Key
Mood
Style
Instrument
Name
Song Kit
Date

Figure 2.25 Categories for filtering your loops.

One extra comment on the Library: You'll see that there are columns such as Tempo, Bars, Signature, Key, and so on. If you click on any of these words, Mixcraft will sort your loops according to the column you have selected.

Understanding Extra Icons, Menus, and Settings

You may wish to familiarize yourself with the icons you see at the top of the screen, as shown in Figure 2.26.

Figure 2.26   Icons at the top of the Mixcraft screen.

You don't necessarily need these right away, but if you hover your mouse over each icon, you will see a tooltip telling you what each icon does.

Below those icons, you'll see three other buttons, as shown in Figure 2.27.

Figure 2.27   Additional buttons near the top of the screen.

One of these buttons is labeled Marker. It's worth explaining what a marker does. This is for marking up certain sections of your song with names such as verse, chorus, and so on. Click somewhere along the timeline of your song with your mouse. You'll see the green flag appear. Then click on the Marker button, and you'll see the dialog box shown in Figure 2.28.

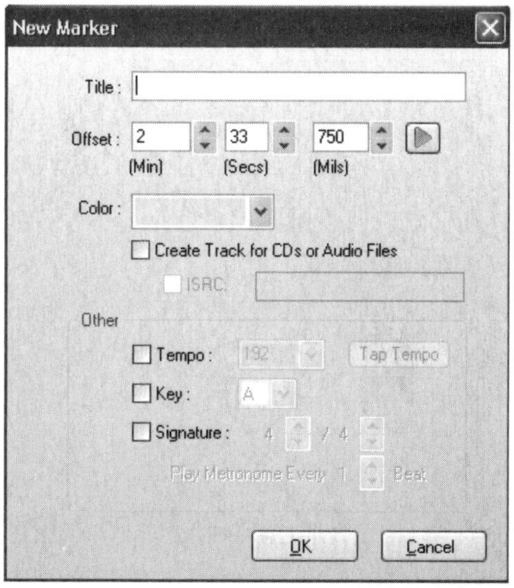

Figure 2.28   Dialog box for adding a new marker.

You can use the marker for simple naming, but you'll see that it also has more extensive uses, such as inserting tempo, key, or time-signature changes in the middle of the song, and it's also used for marking up audio if you want to split a long region into tracks for exporting tracks from a live concert to a CD.

When you have created a marker point, you can drag it to the left or right in the time-line using the mouse, and you can double-click on a marker to edit it.

You'll also see a button at the top of the screen that says Clip Volume, as shown in Figure 2.29.

Figure 2.29 The Clip Volume button toward the top of the screen.

This is mostly for more advanced audio editing purposes.

The icon next to it, Snap to Measure, is useful, and it controls how your mouse behaves as you move around a song (see Figure 2.30).

Figure 2.30 The Snap to Measure button toward the top of the screen.

Click on this and you'll see the choices shown in Figure 2.31.

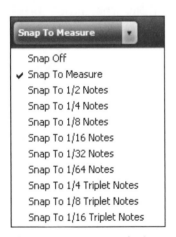

Figure 2.31 Snap choices.

It may be set to Snap to Measure. To see this feature in action, you may need to zoom in very close on your song. (Choose the plus button to do this.) See whether you can zoom all the way down to the bar level in your song. (Make sure Beats is selected at the top of your screen, rather than Time.)

Now try dragging a region to the right or left, and you should notice that the region will only snap to the nearest measure or bar (if that is what your Snap value says). Experiment with this setting to see the importance of it as a tool when editing.

Incidentally, you can also investigate the menus at the very top of the Mixcraft screen at this time (see Figure 2.32), although the specific features you'll need will be covered as and when you need to use them.

Figure 2.32   The menus in Mixcraft.

Also notice the master volume control to the right of the display counter, as shown in Figure 2.33.

Figure 2.33   The main volume display for Mixcraft.

You can drag this left or right to alter the volume of the song.

Notice the little icons to the immediate right of the main display counter, as shown in Figure 2.34.

Figure 2.34   Icons to the right of the main display counter.

You can click on these to activate features such as the metronome and to alter the tempo of the project and so on. Once again, use these carefully and sparingly!

You can also turn off the display of any of the settings windows at the bottom of your screen (and free up screen real estate) by locating the small minus button toward the bottom right, next to the word Undock (see Figure 2.35).

Figure 2.35   Icon to turn off the Details screen at the bottom.

When you hide all the tabs at the bottom, the same icon changes its appearance to a plus button. Click on this if you wish to retrieve the view of any of the tabs at the bottom of the screen.

Starting a New Song in Mixcraft

Press Ctrl+N (or click the New Project icon or go to File > New Project). Mixcraft will ask you to save your previous project first, as shown in Figure 2.36.

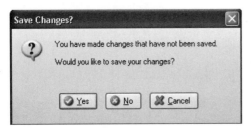

Figure 2.36 Dialog box when you close a project without saving.

The New Song window will appear with three choices. The first option (Record Yourself or Your Band) is the one you would choose if you were planning to record fresh audio (or import audio); see Figure 2.37.

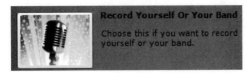

Figure 2.37 The first choice when you start a new project.

The third option (Build Virtual Instrument Tracks) is the one you would choose if you were planning to create MIDI data by playing in from a keyboard or entering notes by typing or clicking them in, using what are called *virtual instruments* (see Figure 2.38).

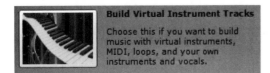

Figure 2.38 The option for choosing virtual instruments (MIDI).

The middle option (Build Loop & Beat Matched Music) is the one you would choose if you were planning to build a song using the loops provided with Mixcraft (see Figure 2.39).

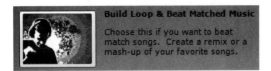

Figure 2.39 The option for working with loops.

The middle option is the one you should choose first. Bear in mind, incidentally, that any Mixcraft project can have a mixture of all three of these kinds of tracks. At this stage, it's mostly a question of Mixcraft choosing an appropriate template for you.

When you have chosen the loops option, a new song screen is displayed, most likely with eight Audio tracks (all empty of regions at this stage). If you don't want as many as eight Audio tracks, click on any track (on the left, where you see its name) and go to Track > Delete Track (via the main menu at the top of the screen). You may wish to restrict the number of tracks if necessary.

You may also want to set the speed of the song, as well as the key and time signature. This is best done from the Project tab you see at the bottom of the screen. It's wise to choose this now, before you import any loops, although you can alter this later, and the loops will change their speed and behavior if you do. See Figure 2.40.

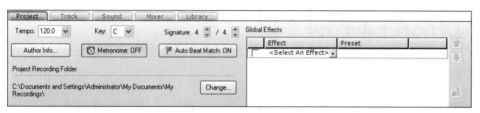

Figure 2.40 The Project tab at the bottom of the Mixcraft screen.

Now click on the Library tab at the bottom of the screen, audition and filter the loops you may need, and when you have found something suitable, you can drag it onto the timeline (in one of the song's tracks).

Don't forget the Category box on the left-hand side, which allows you to select the instrument you're looking for (not just drums!). See Figure 2.41.

Figure 2.41 The Category choices for filtering loops.

When you drag the first loop into the song, you may well get the message shown in Figure 2.42.

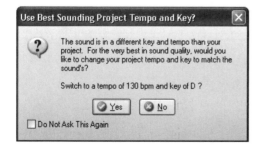

Figure 2.42 Warning message when dragging a loop into your project.

You then need to choose whether to fit the song's tempo around the speed of the loop you have chosen or vice versa. Clearly all the loops will need to conform to some kind of agreed-upon tempo, or else the song will sound very strange and disjointed. Mixcraft will then tend to stick with the initial choice you have made.

As you drag in loops, it's a good idea to keep each loop on a different track, as each may need different treatment in terms of looping, editing, effects, and so on.

Use the skills you have already learned to edit and alter the regions.

Saving and Exporting Your Song

Once the project is completed (including setting the levels correctly), you can export your work using the menu shown in Figure 2.43.

Figure 2.43 Choices that appear when you choose to mix down your project.

This will render your complete song as a stereo file that can be played on anyone's computer or burned as a disc. MP3 and WAV are probably the best-known formats. A wave file (WAV) is an uncompressed version of the music, and an MP3 file is compressed in size, so it easier to email to people as an attachment or upload to a website. Bear in mind, though, that saving as an MP3 file slightly reduces the quality, and you cannot uncompress an MP3 file later.

3 Getting Started with GarageBand: Skills Acquisition

This chapter will help get you familiar with the settings, screens, and buttons in GarageBand and enable you to acquire skills that you will apply to the lessons in the book.

There is a video on the disc accompanying these materials that follows these same steps, if you prefer to watch rather than read.

These materials are intended for use with GarageBand '11 (part of the iLife '11 suite) or GarageBand '09 (part of the iLife '09 suite).

There are earlier versions of GarageBand available, and some of these materials will work with earlier versions, but we recommend upgrading to the latest version if possible.

Starting GarageBand

Look on your computer for the Guitar icon, which may be on the Dock of your Mac (see Figure 3.1). Alternatively, you can navigate to the hard drive, choose Applications, and select GarageBand from there.

When you first turn on GarageBand, the software may display the last song you happened to be working on. In this case, though, we want to see exactly what the software looks like to a beginner, so choose File > New. You'll see the window shown in Figure 3.2.

Notice that GarageBand gives you several options on this screen, some of which we won't cover in this book.

Learn to Play and Lesson Store are both excellent and worth discovering, and they focus chiefly on acquiring piano and guitar skills.

Magic GarageBand is a very useful feature if you want to find out how certain instrumental combinations and musical styles work. In fact, this can also lead you straight into composing, but we shan't focus on that. iPhone Ringtone is also slightly off topic when you are first learning GarageBand.

Figure 3.1   GarageBand desktop icon.

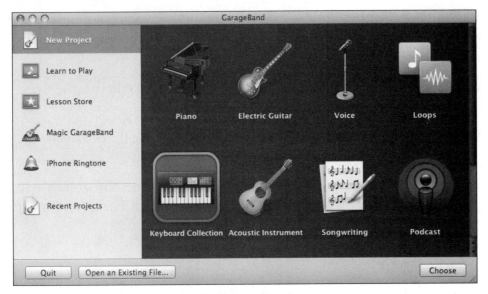

Figure 3.2   New project screen in GarageBand.

What is perhaps most useful right away is to look at an example song that comes with GarageBand, so instead of choosing to start a new project (we'll do that later in this guide), choose File > Open and navigate the path shown in Figure 3.3 on your Mac.

Notice that you should have a folder called GarageBand Demo Songs. Choose the first one, which is called Daydream. If you cannot locate this folder, you can open another GarageBand song you may have created. Alternatively, you can do an online search for the phrase "GarageBand demo songs" to see what you can find and perhaps download.

When you have opened the song, the screen should look like what you see in Figure 3.4.

The Preferences Box

Before you play or edit the song, now is a good time to familiarize yourself with the settings inside GarageBand. Go to GarageBand > Preferences, and the dialog box shown in Figure 3.5 will appear.

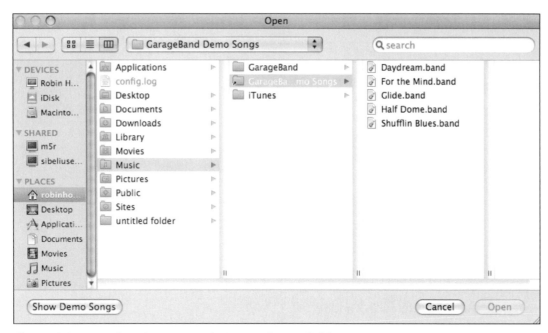

Figure 3.3   Locating GarageBand's Demo Songs folder.

Figure 3.4   A GarageBand project (Daydream, a demo song).

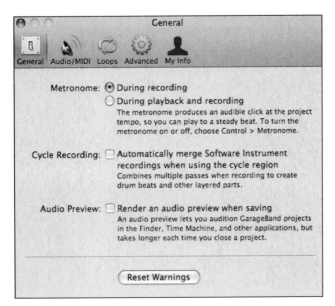

Figure 3.5 GarageBand's Preferences window.

Notice the five choices along the top, starting with General.

On this first tab, you can leave the settings as you find them. The metronome should be on during recording only, and the other boxes shouldn't be checked.

The second tab, Audio/MIDI, is where GarageBand will "see" whatever external devices you may have connected to your machine, under Audio Output and Audio Input (see Figure 3.6).

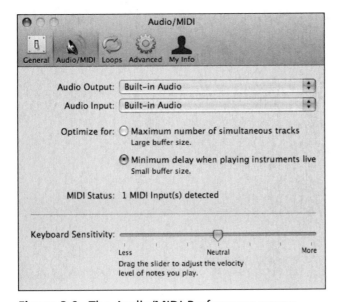

Figure 3.6 The Audio/MIDI Preferences screen.

If you have an audio interface or a MIDI device, such as a keyboard, connected to your computer, GarageBand should detect this, and your screen may look more like what you see in Figure 3.7.

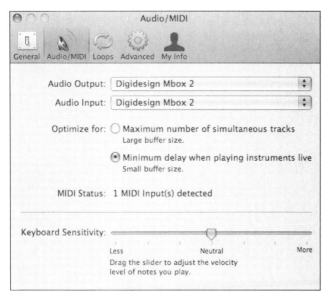

Figure 3.7 Audio/MIDI settings with an external audio interface present.

If you make a change to your device, GarageBand will spend a few seconds initializing the audio drivers it needs. Generally speaking, it is a very good idea to acquire an audio interface if you are working with GarageBand, because this allows you to record sound with quality and clarity, rather than using your Mac's built-in microphone and digital converter.

The third tab, Loops, has various choices. Again, you may wish to leave the settings as you find them. The same applies for the Advanced and My Info tabs. Close that floating screen when you are finished setting your preferences.

Playback

Now you might want to test that playback is working on your computer. Locate the main playback controls on the screen, as shown in Figure 3.8.

Figure 3.8 The main playback controls in GarageBand.

These include all the standard controls, including Rewind to the Beginning and so forth. Click on the main Play button (or tap the spacebar on your computer) to initiate and stop playback.

When you press Stop or the spacebar, you'll notice that GarageBand's main play cursor (the play head) remains where you stopped it, as shown in Figure 3.9.

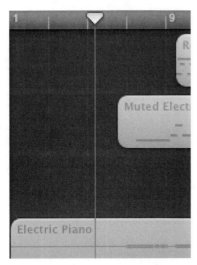

Figure 3.9   The GarsgeBand play head cursor/line.

To play the song from a specific point, you can drag that play-head cursor with the white triangle that you see at the top of the screen (and in Figure 3.10) to the left or right along the timeline.

Figure 3.10   The top of the play head cursor, which you can move.

Or you can click on the Rewind button on the main transport controls at the bottom. To the left of Rewind is the button that rewinds all the way to the beginning of your song, as shown in Figure 3.11.

Figure 3.11   The Rewind controls.

If you ever get an error message like you see in Figure 3.12, you may wish to follow the advice and perhaps change the settings in GarageBand, as your computer might not have quite enough memory or processing power to play all the tracks simultaneously.

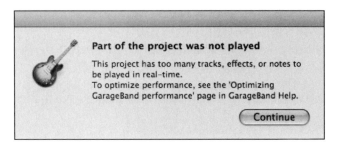

Figure 3.12 Error message on playback.

You can usually slightly reduce the quality of playback to solve this issue—although often simply rebooting your computer can speed things up and solve any issues you may be having!

Understanding Track Layout and Settings

Click on the first track on the left-hand side of the screen. (It will probably turn green.) Notice the volume controls on each track, as shown in Figure 3.13.

Figure 3.13 The display and volume control for each track.

Altering these will allow you to change the relative balance between tracks.

Also locate the panning knob for each track, as shown in Figure 3.14.

Figure 3.14 The panning circle for each track.

Clicking and dragging your mouse up and down should allow you to change the pan from left to right. (We are talking here about the stereo spectrum, and this becomes quite noticeable if you are listening to playback either through headphones [recommended in a lab] or through a pair of loudspeakers.)

You'll also notice a set of icons on each track, as shown in Figure 3.15.

Figure 3.15 The track icons.

One general point worth knowing (and one that is true for almost all software): If you hold your mouse cursor over any button without clicking, the software will usually tell you what the button does. Try that with these icons to learn what each button does. You probably don't want to press on the red Record button at this stage, though!

Locate the buttons for Solo and Mute and experiment with them, as well as with the volume and panning options.

Locking a track will prevent it from being edited, which is useful when you have a track in "perfect" condition. That way, you won't change it in error.

Now take a look at the Automation icon, which is the farthest to the right of these icons. When you click on this, an extra automation screen will open, as shown in Figure 3.16.

Figure 3.16 The automation settings for each track.

The Automation button is very useful for making volume and panning changes to a track while it plays, because you can draw these changes into the track using pointer marks and the mouse, but the whole automation screen can be hidden at this stage if you're a beginner to GarageBand.

Notice the color of each track. If you have the Daydream song loaded, you'll notice that the first two tracks are green, but the rest are blue. These colors help denote what kind of a track each one is. Remember this coloration scheme that you see.

A green track is a MIDI-based Virtual Instrument track. The track was generated using a MIDI instrument (probably a keyboard), and it plays using virtual sounds that are inside the software. These tracks are meant to sound "real," but they are in fact synthetic.

A blue track is an actual Audio track. (It contains real sound waves that have been recorded at some stage.)

GarageBand mixes these two kinds of tracks seamlessly. If you look closely along the timeline, you may also notice that the green tracks' data looks a little different from the blue tracks' data. The green tracks' data looks more like events, and the blue tracks' data looks like sound waves.

Also notice the pictures to the far left of each track. These help denote which sound each track is using. See Figure 3.17.

Figure 3.17 The picture icons displayed on each track.

You can change the sound of a green MIDI track in GarageBand, and you can change some aspects of a blue audio track in GarageBand as well, but audio cannot be modified in the same way as MIDI.

You can drag the regions of any track into another track that has another sound loaded (something to try in a minute). A *region* is the data you see running across the timeline (see Figure 3.18).

Figure 3.18 A GarageBand region.

You'll see that the regions in the song all have different lengths. You can actually drag these regions to the left or right. Be careful here, though: If you move a region, it will definitely affect the sound of your song's playback! Now is a good time to learn the Undo feature in GarageBand, which is Command+Z. (The Command key is the key to the left of the spacebar, perhaps with a picture of an Apple on it.)

The Control Menu

Take a look at the Control menu in GarageBand, shown in Figure 3.19.

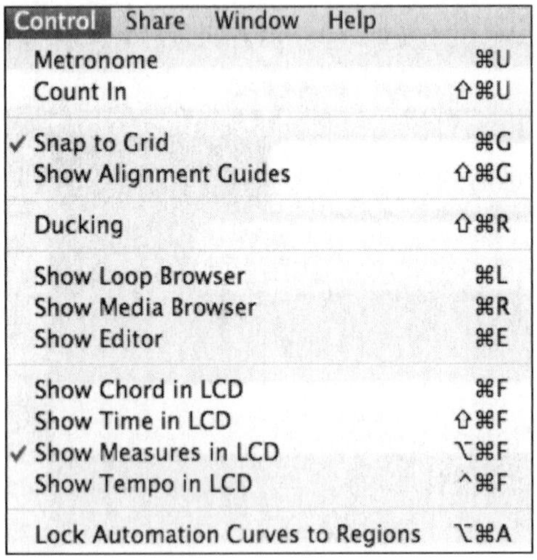

Figure 3.19   The Control menu in GarageBand.

Three very good shortcuts listed here turn off or on certain extra windows in the software:

■ **Command+L.** This will show or hide the Loop Browser, which has lots of musical material to use while you're composing. Try turning this off and on.

■ **Command+R.** This will show or hide the Media Browser, which is the window from which you can select other kinds of music and media to use in your songs, such as movies, audio, and so forth. Try turning this off and on.

■ **Command+E.** This will show or hide the Edit window, which is very useful for when you need to cut or work closely on something in your song. Turn this on. If you don't select a region, nothing will be displayed. If you do select a region, you'll see what's shown in Figure 3.20 if you select a green track's region.

You're viewing MIDI data. If you then select a blue track's region, you'll see what's shown in Figure 3.21.

These are really important screens that we'll discuss much more.

Figure 3.20 The MIDI Edit screen in GarageBand.

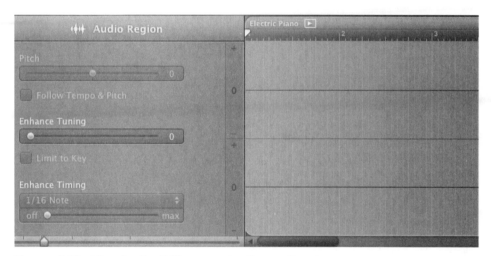

Figure 3.21 The Audio Edit screen in GarageBand.

You can also double-click on any region to open the Edit window—that might be an even easier thing to remember. Remember the shortcut to hide this window if you don't need to do any editing.

The Track Menu

Take a look at the Track menu, shown in Figure 3.22, which is also important.

This gives you more specific options for what to do with individual tracks in your song. Once again, try and learn the shortcuts.

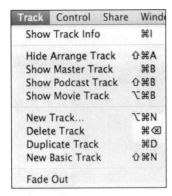

Figure 3.22 The Track menu in GarageBand.

Use Command+I if you want to know how a specific track in your song was first generated or change details about that track. Select one of your tracks on the left-hand side (where the track name is). With Track Info selected, you can find out more detail. This screen will vary, depending on whether you chose a blue or a green track. If you chose a green MIDI track, this is the place where you can choose a different sound for your MIDI data from the list that appears, as shown in Figure 3.23.

Figure 3.23 Track info for a MIDI/Virtual Instrument track.

Once again, remember the shortcut to hide this window.

The Arrange Track, which can also be activated from the Track menu (shortcut: Command+Shift+A), opens or closes a small extra timeline at the top of the screen, which allows you to choose part of your song as the verse or the chorus, and so on.

If you activate the Arrange Track and then click and drag along that very line, something like what you see in Figure 3.24 will happen.

Figure 3.24 Viewing the Arrange feature in GarageBand.

Using the example in Figure 3.24, you can click on the name "untitled 1" and rename this section "Verse," "Chorus," "Section A," and so on. And in fact, you can drag all of your sections around very easily with your mouse to radically alter the format of your song. But all the music that GarageBand finds during that section will move, so be careful!

Hide the Arrange Track if you need, using the shortcut Command+Shift+A. Undo any actions if necessary. (Remember, Command+Z is the shortcut.)

The Master Track (shortcut: Command+B) brings up a separate track in your song, usually at the bottom, that controls the overall volume of your song. In the example song Daydream, it looks like what you see in Figure 3.25.

Figure 3.25 Viewing the Master Track in GarageBand.

Notice that there's no music on this track, just a solid volume line. You can click on this line to make points that you can drag up or down to alter the overall volume of the song. (Be careful if you do this!)

You can turn on a podcast and a movie track, respectively, in GarageBand using the following shortcuts:

- **Shift+Command+B.** This turns on a podcast track for adding pictures when recording a voice-based program. (See Chapter 11, "Creating Podcasts in GarageBand.")

- **Option+Command+B.** This turns on a movie track for adding a movie and becoming a film composer by creating your own soundtrack. (See Chapter 13, "Working with Video in GarageBand.")

You can't have both a podcast track and a movie track in a GarageBand song. You'll notice that extra windows appear when you choose either of these options—GarageBand is guessing that you might want to go and hunt for media to use in your podcast or movie track.

Hide either of these tracks if they're on display—you won't need them right away.

If any extra windows that you didn't expect to see are now displayed on the right-hand side, remember that the Track menu and the Control menu are most likely where you can disable them. Or you can use the shortcuts you have learned! It's always nice to have as much screen real estate as possible, so most of the time your song might look like what you see in Figure 3.26.

Figure 3.26 A GarageBand project with no additional screens open.

Finally, in the Track menu, you'll see that you can add or remove tracks in your song—and there are shortcuts for doing all of these actions, so you don't need to go to the menu each time.

Navigating and Zooming

Look down at the bottom of the screen and you'll see what's shown in Figure 3.27.

Figure 3.27 The Zoom ruler on the GarageBand screen.

Drag the marker on this ruler to the left or right, and you'll see that the song zooms in and out via changes to the timeline at the top of the screen.

Now if you double-click on any region, the Edit window will appear. (Alternatively, you can select a region and type Command+E.) Try it with a region in one of the blue Audio tracks first.

Figure 3.28 The Edit screen (when an audio region is in use).

Notice that this new Edit screen has a zoom ruler at the bottom left. Also notice there's a scroll bar below the orange audio that allows you to scroll through the audio. And notice the little Play button, which allows you to audition just this region, as shown in Figure 3.29.

Figure 3.29 The Play button inside the Audio Edit screen.

Double-clicking on a green MIDI region gives much the same results. Notice that for MIDI, a Piano Roll Editor appears by default, as shown in Figure 3.30.

On the right-hand side, there's a place to vertically scroll down or up to see the pitches being displayed, as shown in Figure 3.31.

You'll also notice that your cursor changes to be a pencil tool as you hover over the data.

Figure 3.30 The Piano Roll Editor inside the MIDI Editor screen.

Figure 3.31 The vertical scroll settings for the Piano Roll Editor.

You can also see a different view of the same data by choosing Score on the left-hand side, as shown in Figure 3.32.

You can obviously edit the MIDI notes by altering the pitches displayed in the Score view or by adding new ones.

Song Display

Take a look at the main time display at the bottom of the screen, as shown in Figure 3.33.

Click on the eighth-note icon, and the window shown in Figure 3.34 will appear.

This gives you choices to display the song in absolute time (minutes and seconds), choose a tuner (if you're about to record live guitar), get information about the

Figure 3.32 The Score View option for the MIDI Edit screen.

Figure 3.33 The main time display or LCD.

Figure 3.34 Display options inside the LCD.

song's key and time signature, and go back to displaying the song in bars and beats (the eighth-note icon).

Other Onscreen Icons

You'll see a couple of other icons at the bottom of the screen, as shown in Figure 3.35. These all replicate skills and features you have already learned.

Figure 3.35 Two icons at the bottom left of the screen.

The icon on the left will add a new track if you click on it, and the icon on the right will show/hide the Track Editor, which we've learned other ways to display.

From left to right, the three icons in Figure 3.36 will display/hide the Loop Browser, the Track Info screen, or the Media Browser.

Figure 3.36 Three icons at the bottom right of the screen.

There's also a main volume control for the whole song, with an LED display that lights up when the score plays, as shown in Figure 3.37.

Figure 3.37 The main volume control and display for your project.

Basic Editing

First of all, as discussed, you can move any of the actual musical material in the song by picking up a region and dragging it with your mouse to the left or right. Try it with any region in the song.

On the subject of editing, though, you'll want to know how to loop an existing piece of music, cut it, and make copies. Taking a look once again at the existing song, if you need to cut or split a region in two, first select a region you'd like to work on and then click on the timeline to position your mouse where you'd like to cut the region. See Figure 3.38.

Figure 3.38 Making a selection on the timeline.

Then type Command+T (or choose Edit > Split), and your region should be cut in two, as shown in Figure 3.39.

Now click away and then reselect one half of that new split region, and you can drag it around or delete it. You may find it easier to open the Edit window to make more

Figure 3.39 A region split in two.

accurate selections for where to split a region. Also bear in mind that this is a very good time to zoom in on regions (when you need to select the correct place in a region for editing).

Now is also a good time to learn about the Snap icon that you see in the top-right corner of the GarageBand screen (see Figure 3.40).

Figure 3.40 The Snap icon.

Click on this icon, and you'll see that you can choose various snap positions for your mouse, as shown in Figure 3.41.

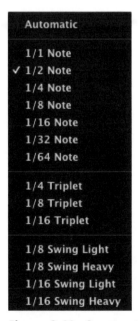

Figure 3.41 Snap options in GarageBand.

These snap choices are important for selecting precisely on a barline, beat, half note, and so on. This will vary according to your needs during the editing process. Try experimenting with changing the snap value, and see how it changes the way the mouse can select points in your song.

You may also notice a small icon on the timeline at the end of the last region in your song, as shown in Figure 3.42.

Figure 3.42 The End of Project icon.

You can drag that marker point to the right or left to denote the end of your project. This may be important when you come to save your whole song as a stereo audio file.

You can copy and paste regions in your song in several ways.

If you are dealing with something that is not a loop (such as an orange audio region), select a region first and then hold down the Option key and drag the region to some empty space. You'll see that GarageBand leaves the original region in place but allows a copy to be made, as shown in Figure 3.43.

Figure 3.43 Making a copy of a region using Option-drag.

The second way of getting any region to repeat or loop is to hold your mouse right at the end of a region in the top-right corner. You should see the cursor change its appearance to a circular-style looping cursor. Drag this to the right to extend any region farther into the timeline of your song. This works for audio or MIDI loops.

As already suggested, you can also drag a region from one actual track to another, but be careful when you do this. Generally, you'll want to keep musical material within the same track. Also, you can't drag an audio region into a MIDI track and vice versa.

One more important point about editing: As we've already pointed out, if you double-click on a region, this should automatically open up the Edit screen at the bottom of the page, as shown in Figure 3.44.

Now you can make what you see down below line up exactly with the region in your score, if you locate the small icon in the bottom right of where all your regions are displayed. It's shown in Figure 3.45; look closely for it.

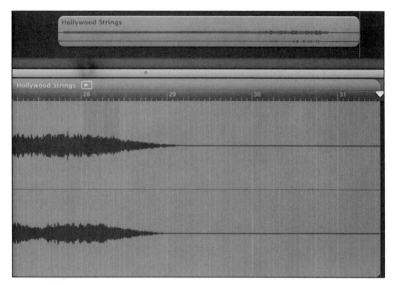

Figure 3.44 The Track Editor (accessed by double-clicking on any region).

Figure 3.45 The Play Head Alignment icon.

Clicking on this to make both tiny arrows line up locks the timeline and editor play heads (to be technical). It means that if you now play your main GarageBand song, the expanded Edit window will play at the same time as the region. We suggest that you always align these two screens by following this step.

More advanced features concerning editing (such as adding effects, enhancing the timing, and working with automation) will be covered in Chapters 5, 7, and 9.

Starting a New Song in GarageBand

To start a brand-new GarageBand project (which has the file extension .band), just type Command+N while you're running GarageBand (or go to File > New), and you'll first be asked whether you want to save your previous project, as shown in Figure 3.46.

Figure 3.46 Error message if you close a project without saving it.

A new window will appear. If you're about to start working with the internal loops in GarageBand, you'll want to choose the Loops icon, shown in Figure 3.47.

Figure 3.47   The Loops option when you start a new project.

You'll then be asked to give your new project a name and choose a location for where it will be saved, as well as to select your tempo, key signature, and time signature (see Figure 3.48).

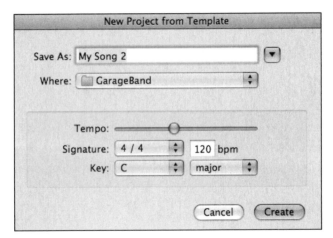

Figure 3.48   Naming, saving, and setting up your new project.

You can alter these musical choices later if you wish, by making changes in the LCD display of your project. If you're ready, click OK, and a new project (song) will be created.

The new screen looks a little different from the previous song you were working on (see Figure 3.49).

There are no tracks yet chosen, and the Loop Browser has been opened by default on the right-hand side.

Now it's time to audition and select loops from the large library available. There are a lot to choose from! First, you can click on the Scale drop-down menu, as shown in Figure 3.50.

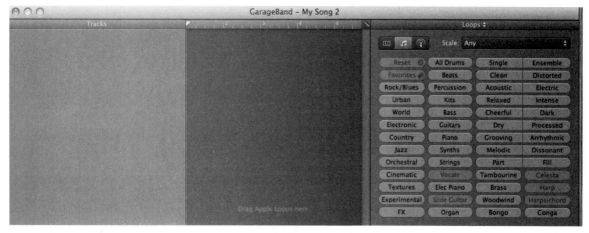

Figure 3.49 A new loop project before any tracks have been added.

Figure 3.50 The Scale option in the Loop Browser.

This gives you the chance to restrict the loops according to specific scales.

You can just click on a particular genre, such as Jazz, and the potential loops you can use will be displayed below, as shown in Figure 3.51.

Name	Tempo	Key	Beats	Fav
44th Street Long	–	–	00:39	
44th Street Medium	–	–	00:19	
44th Street Short	–	–	00:13	
Blue Jazz Organ Riff 01	136	C	8	
Blue Jazz Organ Riff 02	136	C	16	
Blue Jazz Organ Riff 03	136	C	8	
Blue Jazz Organ Riff 04	136	C	8	
Blue Jazz Organ Riff 06	136	C	8	
Blue Jazz Organ Riff 07	136	C	16	
Blue Jazz Piano 01	136	C	16	
Blue Jazz Piano 02	136	C	16	
Bossa Lounger Long	–	–	00:32	
Bossa Lounger Medium	–	–	00:13	

Figure 3.51 Blue and green jazz loops.

Blue loops are audio loops, and green loops are MIDI-based loops (see Figure 3.52). Both are valid, but they will behave and be edited in slightly different ways.

Figure 3.52 The icons that denote audio or MIDI loops.

If you click on any loop, it will start playing (and actually loop around).

Audition what you need and then simply drag the loop across to where the empty tracks are. GarageBand will create a brand-new track automatically, as shown in Figure 3.53.

Figure 3.53 A MIDI jazz loop dragged into a project.

You can then continue to add new loops. (Drag extra loops into different tracks for each new sound you want to create.) Don't forget the shortcut Command+L to open or close the Loop Browser. Then start using the skills you have already acquired to build your song and edit it.

Saving and Exporting Your Song

Once the project is completed (including setting the levels correctly and ensuring it plays back exactly as you would like), you can always export your work using the menu shown in Figure 3.54.

Figure 3.54 The Share menu in GarageBand.

This will render your complete song as a stereo file that can be played on anyone's computer or burned as a disc. Garage Band will then give you the window shown in Figure 3.55.

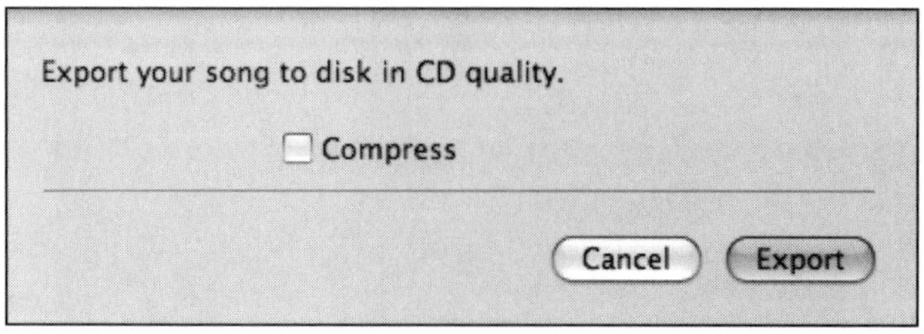

Figure 3.55 Exporting your song as a stereo file.

You can choose to check the box that says Compress or not. Leaving this unchecked will create an AIF file, which is an uncompressed version of the music, and checking the box will create an MP3 file, which is easier to email to people as an attachment or upload to a website. Bear in mind, though, that saving as an MP3 file slightly reduces the quality of the file, and you cannot later uncompress an MP3 file.

If you then click on Export, the window shown in Figure 3.56 will appear, asking you to name and save the file and determine where it will be saved.

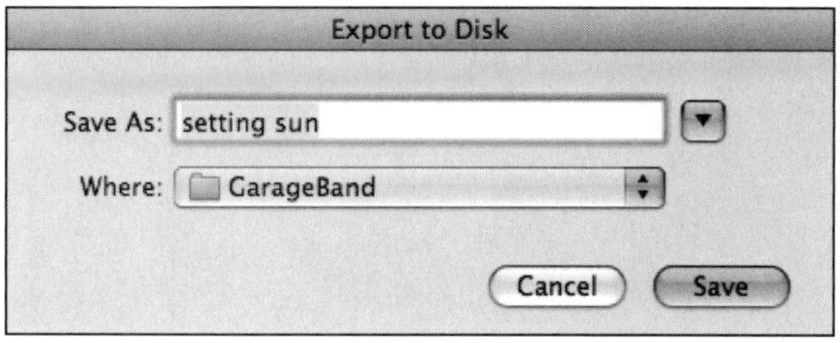

Figure 3.56 Saving your exported stereo audio file.

4 Getting Started with Mixcraft

This chapter contains two lessons to help you get started with Mixcraft.

Lesson 1: A Beginning, a Middle, and an End
by Richard McCready

National Standards

4. Composing and arranging music within specified guidelines

Objectives

- Create music using the included loops in Mixcraft.

- Audition loops and add them to the Sequencer window.

- Balance the sounds of your loops using the Mixer window.

Class Time Required

You should be able to complete this lesson well in two one-hour sessions.

Materials

- Computer with Mixcraft installed

- Internet connection

- Headphones or monitor speakers

You will find an example of a completed project on the companion DVD. Look for a file titled Begin Middle End.mx5 and an MP3 file titled Begin Middle End Mixdown .mp3.

Procedure

1. Make sure you have read through Chapter 2, "Getting Started with Mixcraft."

2. Launch Mixcraft and select the middle option (Build Loop & Beat-Matched Music) from the New Project screen. It is a good idea to save your song every few minutes as you go through the project. You can do so easily by clicking the Save button (it has a picture of a floppy disk on it) or by selecting File > Save. You can also use the shortcut key combination Ctrl+S. The first time you save to disk, you will have to give your song a name.

3. In the lower part of the screen, the Details section, select the Library tab. This is where you can access hundreds of loops from within Mixcraft.

4. Look for some rhythmic loops first of all. Drums are always good to start with when creating music. On the right side of the loop Library screen, you'll see a drop-down option for Category. Select Instrument as your sort category and then select Drums in the panel below. You'll now see many different drum loops listed on the right in the Library. As you click on the play head (the blue triangle) beside any of these loops, they will download from the Internet (which is why you need an Internet connection when working in Mixcraft), and you will hear the loops play in your headphones or monitor speakers. Audition any loops that have a length of 1, 2, or 4 in the #bars column. Keep auditioning until you find one you like for the beginning of your music.

5. Click the yellow plus sign beside the name of the loop you chose, and the loop will appear in the first available track in the Sequencer window. If you see a dialog box that asks you whether you wish to switch the tempo of your song to the tempo of the loop you selected, click Yes, and your song will now follow the exact tempo (speed) of the loop you chose.

   You can also drag the loop into the Sequencer window by grabbing the name of the loop with your mouse and dragging it upward. A vertical line will show you where your loop is going. Make sure you drop it in the first available track, at the beginning of the song. If you drop it in the wrong place, you can always grab its name bar (what we're calling the "scruff of the neck" in this book) and move it to the right place.

6. Now that you have the first loop in your song, you'll notice that across the top of the loop you have a play triangle (click it and you hear the loop), a Loop Repeat button (click it and the loop duplicates), and the loop name ("the scruff of the neck"). Underneath that you see the waveform of the loop. That's what the loop looks like in digital audio. In a drum loop you will see many spikes—these are the loud hits in the waveform. The spikes tell you how loud the music is—the bigger the spike, the louder the hit. Experienced audio engineers can tell what a loop sounds like just by looking at the waveform!

   Duplicate the loop until it goes all the way from the beginning of the song to the number 5 (the end of the fourth measure). You won't have to do this if you already selected a loop that lasts four measures.

7. Return to the loop Library and find another drum beat to go with your first selected loop. Find something that contrasts with the one you first chose. You can add this new loop to the song at Measure 5. Click on the dash just below the number 5 on the timeline. (A vertical line will now appear at that point.) Drag the loop into the Sequencer and place it at number 5 in the first track, right beside the loop you already put in. Duplicate this loop until it goes to the number 9 (the end of the eighth measure).

8. Choose a third drum loop from the Library. Drag it to the Sequencer at Measure 9 and duplicate it until it reaches the number 13 (the end of the twelfth measure). Now click the Rewind to Beginning button (or hit the Home key on your keyboard) and then click the Play button (or hit the spacebar) to hear how the three drum beats you chose sound consecutively. Click Stop or hit the spacebar again to stop playback. If you change your mind about a drum loop, you can get rid of it. Highlight it in the Sequencer by clicking its name, press Delete on your keyboard, and then choose a different loop to replace it.

9. In the Category option in the loop Library, change from Drums to Bass. Audition some bass sounds. Choose one to go with your first four measures and add it into the Sequencer, but make sure you choose a loop that lasts 1, 2, or 4 bars. (Check the number in the #bars column.) If you see a dialog box that asks you whether you wish to switch the key of your song to the key of the loop you selected, click Yes, and your song will now follow the same key of the loop you chose.

   Make sure you don't drop the bass loop on top of the drum beat—put it in the next track down. Duplicate it so it lasts as long as the drum beat in the beginning section (up to the number 5 on the timeline). Listen to the first four measures and make changes if you don't like the bass and drums together. Add different bass loops in for the middle section, Measures 5–8 (up to the number 9 on the timeline), and the end section, Measures 9–12 (up to the number 13).

10. In the Category option in the loop Library, change from Bass to Guitar. By now you should be getting really good at adding loops to the Sequencer. Add a guitar line so you have different loops for the beginning, the middle, and the end of your song. Make sure your loops are 1, 2, or 4 measures long and don't overlap into other sections. Keep listening all the time to see whether you like how the loops fit together.

11. Add another instrument to your song. Change the category from Guitar to something different (your choice now). Add in loops in the three sections of the song.

12. Now select the Mixer tab. As you listen to your song, use the volume faders to adjust the relative volume of each track so that each instrument is equally

audible. It's easier to mix if you set the song to loop—that way, you don't have to keep restarting the song every time it plays through. To set the song to loop, look in the green display counter where the time code is displayed and click on the loop arrow. Mixcraft will select all 12 measures of the song to loop automatically.

Use the L-R sliders above the volume faders to adjust where your instruments are from left to right in the mix. Imagine where you would like them to be on stage as they would be in live performance and then reflect this by mixing them to the appropriate side in the mix.

You can adjust the Hi, Mid, and Lo response in each track by turning the knobs in the EQ section of the Mixer. As you mix, make sure that the volume levels do not light up the red warning light at the top of the volume faders. If this happens, you must bring down the volume fader, or it will sound distorted in the final mixdown.

You should check volume levels every time you change a pan position (L-R) or EQ setting, as even small alterations will affect the output level of the track. It is important to get a strong volume signal without lighting the red warning light. Keep your Main Mix fader down fairly low until you have eliminated all red lights in the instrument faders, and then you'll find you have some room to boost the Main Mix level. You'll learn many skills of mixing as you work through this book, but for now your most important task is to avoid the red lights.

13.   When you feel that your song is the best you can make it and when the volume indicators never go into the red, click on the button to mix your song down to an audio file (it looks like an arrow pointing to a sheet of paper) or select File > Mix Down To > MP3.

If Mixcraft asks whether you would like to save your changes before mixing down, click Yes. Select a location for your mixed-down song and save it as an MP3 version. That way, you'll be able to listen to your song on your iPod or other MP3 player or use it as a ringtone on your phone. Make sure to play your song to friends or family members to see whether they like it.

Extensions

After you have mastered making a song with a beginning, a middle, and an end in 12 measures, make another song with 24 measures (eight measures per section). This will allow you to use some of the longer loops. Also, try adding in more than four instruments to the song, but still start with drums, then bass, then guitar. You should also look ahead to Chapter 17 for ways to put your song online so other people can listen to it.

Lesson 2: AABA Rock *by Richard McCready*

National Standards

4. Composing and arranging music within specified guidelines

Objectives

- Use loops in Mixcraft to create a piece in ternary form, in which the music returns to original material after a bridge section.

- Split loops in Mixcraft.

- Use markers.

- Add digital effects to the master mix.

Class Time Required

You should be able to complete this lesson well in two one-hour sessions.

Materials

- Computer with Mixcraft installed

- Internet connection

- Headphones or monitor speakers

You will find an example of a completed project on the companion DVD. Look for a file titled AABA Rock.mx5 and an MP3 file titled AABA Rock Mixdown.mp3.

Procedure

1. Make sure you have read through Chapter 2, on getting started with Mixcraft.

2. Launch Mixcraft and select the middle option (Build Loop & Beat-Matched Music) from the New Project screen. Remember to save your song every few minutes as you go through the project.

3. In the lower part of the screen, the Details section, select the Library tab.

4. Look for the Category drop-down option on the right side of the loop Library screen. Select Style as your sort category and then choose a musical style for your song in the panel below. You'll now see loops in that musical style listed on the right in the Library. Click on the play head (the blue triangle) beside any of these loops and audition some of them. Find a drum beat or other rhythmic pattern with which to begin your song.

5. Click the yellow plus sign beside the name of the loop you chose, and it will appear in the first available track in the Sequencer window. If you see a dialog

box that asks you whether you wish to switch the tempo of your song to the tempo of the loop you selected, click Yes, and your song will now follow the exact tempo (speed) of the loop you chose.

You can also drag the loop into the Sequencer window by grabbing the name of the loop with your mouse and dragging it upward. A vertical line will show you where your loop is going. Make sure you drop it in the first available track, at the beginning of the song. If you drop it in the wrong place, you can always grab its name bar (the "scruff of the neck") and move it to the right place.

6. The first section of your song will be 16 measures long, so if you have chosen a loop that lasts 16 measures, you don't have to duplicate it. If your loop is shorter than 16 measures, duplicate it until it fills the track up to the number 17 (the end of the sixteenth measure) on the timeline. If your drum loop is longer than 16 measures, you will need to cut it to fit. Click in the loop's title bar at the point where you want to cut the loop and select Edit > Split. You could also use the shortcut key combination Ctrl+T, or you can right-click on the loop right under the number 17 and select Split from the drop-down menu. Now select the second half of the newly split region by clicking the loop's name bar and select Edit > Delete or press Delete on the keyboard.

7. Move the horizontal scroll bar to the right so you can see numbers 25–33 on the timeline. Drag the same drum beat (the one you used at the beginning of the song) from the loop Library into the first track so it begins at Measure 25. You may need to duplicate it so it fills up the track to the number 33 (the end of the 32nd measure). If your drum beat is longer than eight measures, you will need to cut it to fit.

Click in the loop's title bar at the point where you want to cut the loop and select Edit > Split. You could also use the shortcut key combination Ctrl+T, or you can right-click on the loop right under the number 33 and select Split from the drop-down menu. Now select the second half of the newly split region by clicking the loop's name bar and select Edit > Delete or press Delete on the keyboard.

8. Move the horizontal scroll bar to the left so you can see Measures 17–32. There should be a gap in your drum beat at this point. Select a new drum beat and drag it from the Loop Browser to fill the gap. If the loop is shorter than eight measures, you will have to duplicate it. If it is longer than eight measures, you will have to cut it. There is no need for alarm if the loop you drag in covers something you've already added. When you split and delete the part you don't need, you will see the underneath loop again.

9. You have now created an AABA structure in your drum loops track—eight measures of A repeated (16 measures), eight measures of B, and eight measures

of A again. We call this *ternary form*, as it has three distinct sections—an opening, a bridge, and then a return to the opening material.

It helps to have markers in a song to see where you are in the structure (this becomes crucial with longer songs), so right-click on the number 1 on the timeline and select Add Marker from the drop-down menu. In the next dialog box, type "A Section" in the Title field, select a color in the Color field, and click OK. You will now see a colored marker flag in the timeline where the A section starts.

Add a marker for "A Section Repeated" at Measure 9, "B Section" at Measure 17, and "A Section Return" at Measure 25. You can use the color option to color-code your sections' marker flags. Now when you are listening to your song, you can use the keyboard shortcuts Ctrl+spacebar to skip forward to the next marker and Ctrl+Shift+spacebar to skip backward to the previous marker. These shortcuts will really help when you're mixing.

10. Audition some bass loops in the Loop Browser. Try to remain within the same Style category if you can. Find a bass loop for the A sections of the song and add that in to Measures 1–16 and 25–32. If you see a dialog box that asks you whether you wish to switch the key of your song to the key of the loop you selected, click Yes, and your song will now follow the same key of the loop you chose.

Find a bass loop for the B section and add that in to Measures 17–24. Cut or duplicate the loops as you need to make them fit into the sections. Listen to your music from the beginning to see whether your loops work well together. Make changes if you need to.

11. Add another instrument to your song. Find some loops you like and add them in to the song. Make sure you keep the AABA structure as you add in the new loops. You can have different instruments in the different sections if you'd like. The AABA Rock example that accompanies this lesson has electric piano in the A sections and electric guitar in the B sections.

12. Now select the Mixer tab. As you listen to your song, use the volume faders to adjust the relative volume of each track so that every instrument is equally audible but does not light the red warning lights at the top of the volume strips. Use the L-R sliders above the volume faders to adjust where your instruments are from left to right in the mix. Imagine where you would like them to be on stage as if it were a live performance and reflect this by mixing them to the appropriate side in the mix. You can adjust the Hi, Mid, and Lo response in each track by turning the knobs in the EQ section of the Mixer.

13. Click on the FX button above the Main Mix fader. This brings up the Global Effects menu, where you can add some digital effects to the overall mix to

thicken up your sound. Select the first slot in the Effect column. (Click the down arrow beside <Select An Effect>.) Select the Classic Compressor. A compressor will even out the sound of your mix by boosting the quiet sounds while keeping the loud sounds in check.

Select one of the presets in the Preset column. (Click the down arrow beside <Preset>.) Most of the presets are self-explanatory. Choose one you think might suit your music. You can see what the compressor looks like by clicking the Edit button. Listen to your music again by pressing the Play button. (You might have to drag the compressor out of the way to get to the Play button.) See whether you can discern a difference as the mix plays through the compressor. If the red light on the compressor turns on, the compressor is working to smooth out your sound.

Click the X in the top-right corner of the compressor to hide it. Even though it is hidden, it will still be working as long as the FX button at the top of the Main Mix fader is selected and the compressor is checked in the Global Effects menu.

14.   Add the Classic Reverb unit to the Global Effects menu for the Main Mix fader. Choose a preset to create the digital effect of re-creating the natural reverberation of a place where your music might be performed. Because music is often recorded in a dry studio with no reverberation, it is really important to add reverb to bring a natural feeling to your mix.

You can see what the reverb unit looks like by clicking the Edit button in the Global Effects menu, and you can close it again by clicking the X in the top-right corner of the reverb unit. Do remember, however, that the reverb unit is still working, even if you can't see it. Also note as you select presets in the Classic Reverb that there is no difference in the versions of presets that have the word (send) after their name—at least, not for the purposes of this project.

15.   Now that you have added effects into the mix, you will need to listen to your song again and check that the red warning light on the Main Mix fader does not light. You will probably find that the optimum level for this master fader is lower than it was before you added in the effects. This does not mean your music is quieter because you have to reduce the master fader—it just means that you no longer have to boost the level as much to ensure a good, full sound. This is a good thing.

When you are satisfied that your song is the best you can make it and that the volume indicators never go into the red, click on the button to mix your song down to an audio file or select File > Mix Down To > MP3. If Mixcraft asks whether you would like to save your changes before mixing down, click Yes.

Select a location for your mixed-down song and save it as an MP3 version. Now you'll be able to listen to your song on your iPod or other MP3 player or use it as a ringtone on your phone. Make sure to play your song for friends or family members to see whether they like it.

Extensions

After you have mastered making a song with an AABA form in 32 measures, make another song with 64 measures (16 measures per section). Also, try adding in more instruments to the song, but still start with drums and bass. You should also look ahead to Chapter 17 for ways to put your song online so other people can listen to it.

5 Getting Started with GarageBand

This chapter contains two lessons to help you get started in GarageBand.

Lesson 1: Loop-dee-Loop *by Michael Fein*

National Standards

3. Improvising melodies, variations, and accompaniments

4. Composing and arranging music within specified guidelines

7. Evaluating music and music performances

Objectives

- Explore the GarageBand Loop Browser

- Import loops into an existing GarageBand project

- Compose a B section using contrasting loops

- Use copy/paste to create an AABA form

- Transpose measures or phrases

Class Time Required

You should be able to complete this lesson well in a one-hour session.

Materials

- Loop-dee-Loop Template file located on the companion DVD

- Example recordings (see Preparations in this lesson for suggested recordings)

Preparations

1. Listen to example recordings from a variety of genres. Count the number of measures in each phrase and notate these on the board. Most songs will have

4-, 8-, or 16-bar phrases. Consider listening to "Fly Me to the Moon" by Frank Sinatra, "She Loves You" by the Beatles, or almost any other pop, jazz, or classical tune.

2. Listen to the example recordings again, this time focusing on the form of the songs. Do the same melody phrases repeat over and over, or can you hear distinctly different sections in the songs? You can describe these different sections using letters: The first section is called A, the next different section is called B, and so forth. How are the A and B sections of the example recordings similar and how are they different? In most cases, the instrumentation will remain the same, but the melodic or harmonic material will change.

Procedure

1. Drag the GarageBand file Loop-dee-Loop Template, located on the companion DVD, onto your computer's hard drive. I suggest storing files on your desktop for easy access.

2. Open Loop-dee-Loop Template in GarageBand.

   Before composing with loops, it is essential that you browse through the available loops in GarageBand and mark your favorites. This will allow you be creative during the composition process.

3. Click on the Loop Browser icon in the bottom toolbar (see Figure 5.1).

Figure 5.1 The Loop Browser icon.

In the Loop Browser, some of the descriptors indicate a style, and some indicate a particular instrument or family of instruments. I suggest avoiding the style descriptors and focusing on the instrument descriptors. In today's modern music, many artists create unique sounds by blending a variety of musical styles and genres to create something altogether new. This is the approach that I prefer to take when composing with loops.

4. Click on a single instrument, such as All Drums. The bottom portion of the Loop Browser will now display a list of hundreds of drum loops available.

Tip: Loops with green icons (see Figure 5.2) next to them are MIDI loops; loops with blue icons (see Figure 5.3) next to them are audio loops. This chapter will focus primarily on using audio, and Chapter 7, "Getting Started with MIDI in GarageBand," will focus primarily on using MIDI. For the purpose of this project, you can use either blue audio loops or green MIDI loops.

Figure 5.2   Green MIDI loop icon.

Figure 5.3   Blue audio loop icon.

5. Click on one of the loops, and it will begin playing. To audition another loop, press the down arrow on your keyboard or click the next loop with your mouse. As you find loops that you like, click the Fav column to place a check mark next to the loop (see Figure 5.4).

Figure 5.4   Click the Fav column to place a check mark next to a loop you like.

6. After auditioning the drum loops, click the Reset button, shown in Figure 5.5, and then repeat this process with other instrument categories.

Figure 5.5   Click the Reset button.

7. After browsing other instruments, click Reset and then click Favorites, as shown in Figure 5.6. The Loop Browser will only display the loops that you marked as favorites in Step 5.

Figure 5.6   Click the Favorites button.

Now that you have an idea of the loops available, let's begin composing!

8. Listen to the file by pressing the spacebar or by clicking the Play button in the bottom toolbar (see Figure 5.7). This bass line is a loop from the GarageBand Loop Browser, and it will serve as the foundation of your loop-based composition.

Figure 5.7   Click the Play button to listen to the file.

9. Click the Cycle button in the bottom toolbar (see Figure 5.8). This puts GarageBand in Cycle mode (also known as *Loop Playback mode*). In Cycle mode, GarageBand will repeat the cycle section infinitely to save you from constantly rewinding and playing the file.

Figure 5.8 Click the Cycle button to repeat a section of the song.

10. Stretch the yellow cycle bar near the top of the screen so it cycles the entire A section from Bar 1 to Bar 9, as shown in Figure 5.9.

Figure 5.9 Stretch the yellow cycle bar from Bar 1 to Bar 9.

11. Press Play and allow GarageBand to cycle the A section.

12. With Favorites still selected in the Loop Browser, click All Drums.

13. Click on various drum loops to audition the drum loop with the bass loop. How do the loops sound together? Does the rhythm work? Continue clicking on drum loops to find one that fits well with the bass loop.

14. When you have found a drum loop that sounds good with the bass loop, drag it into the main Arrange window. GarageBand will automatically create a new track.

15. If the drum loop is fewer than eight full measures, loop out the drum loop audio region so it lasts eight full measures and stops at Measure 9, as shown in Figure 5.10.

Figure 5.10 Loop out the drum loop audio region so it lasts eight full measures and stops at Measure 9.

16. Click All Drums to deselect it in the Loop Browser.

17.   Select another instrument, such as Electric Piano, and audition various electric piano loops to hear whether they work with the bass and drum loop in your composition.

18.   When you have found an electric piano loop, drag it into your composition.

Tip: Instead of using a single loop for eight full bars, try using one loop for four bars and then a similar loop for the next four bars. This adds variety throughout the phrase. For example, try using Deep Electric Piano 01 and then Deep Electric Piano 05, as shown in Figure 5.11.

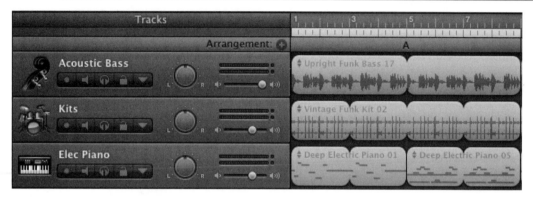

Figure 5.11 Try using Deep Electric Piano 01 for four measures and then Deep Electric Piano 05 for the next four measures.

19.   Select all of the loops in your composition by clicking outside of any loop and dragging across all of your loops. This is called a *rubber-band drag*.

20.   Copy and paste the first A section into the other sections marked A (Bars 9–17 and 25–43), as shown in Figure 5.12.

Figure 5.12 Copy and paste the A section.

Tip: To copy and paste loops, press and hold the Option key and click and drag the loop. You can also use Edit > Copy and Edit > Paste or Command+C and Command+V, but Option-dragging is the most efficient way to copy and paste in GarageBand.

You are now going to compose a B section. This new section should be similar to but different from the A section. (Think back to the A and B sections of the example recordings and how they are similar and different.) If you used Vintage Funk Kit 02 for the drum loop in your A section, try using Vintage Funk Kit 03 for your B section. It usually will sound out of place if your B-section loops are extremely different from your A-section loops. It would also be common to keep the same instrumentation for the B section as you have for the A section. This means that if you have acoustic bass, electric piano, and vintage funk drums for your A section, use those same instruments for your B section.

Tip: Click the double arrow in the upper-left corner of any region to change the selected loop to a different loop from the same category and style. For example, if you click on Upright Funk Bass 17 in the Arrange window, a pop-up window will appear that allows you to change the selected region to a different Upright Funk Bass loop.

---

21.   Drag the yellow cycle bar so it stretches from Bar 17 to Bar 25.

22.   Audition bass loops from the Loop Browser. When you have found one that you think works in the song as a contrast to the first bass loop, drag it into the gray area in the Arrange window, and GarageBand will create a new track. The bass loop for the B section should last from Bars 17 to 25.

23.   Repeat the previous step to add a contrasting drum and electric piano loop, as shown in Figure 5.13.

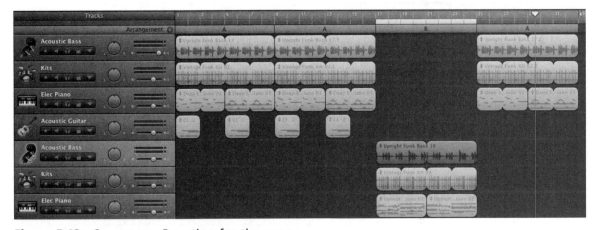

Figure 5.13 Compose a B section for the song.

Transposing regions or phrases can add a lot of interest to your composition. By transposing pitched loops, you can actually change the key center of the selected area of your composition. It is very common to transpose the key of the B section. Common transpositions would be +5 semitones (Perfect 4th interval up) or −5 (Perfect 4th interval down).

24.   Select the pitched loops in your B section. Do not select any drum or percussion loops.

Tip: You can select noncontiguous regions by holding the Command key while you click on regions.

---

25.   Open the Track Editor by clicking on the Scissors icon in the left of the bottom toolbar (see Figure 5.14).

Figure 5.14 The Track Editor icon.

26.   Drag the Pitch slider in the Track Edit window to transpose the pitched loops (see Figure 5.15). Try various settings until you find one that works well with your song. If you change the pitch too much, your loops may sound odd, so try to keep the pitch transposition to somewhere between −5 and +5 and certainly no more than −12 or +12. See Figure 5.16.

Figure 5.15 The Pitch slider, located in the Track Edit window.

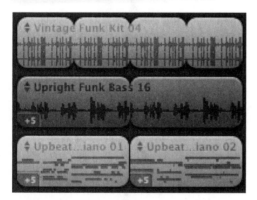

Figure 5.16 Loops transposed up five semitones (+5).

27.   Export the finished project by selecting Share > Send Song to iTunes or Share > Export Song to Disk.

Extensions

Enhance your song by adding percussion loops to the A and B sections. The percussion family includes instruments such as shaker, tambourine, conga, and cowbell. You can also enhance your song by adding additional pitched loops. Consider adding guitar, organ, or strings. As you add additional loops, be careful of the texture of your composition. If you have too many loops playing simultaneously, your song can start to sound too mushy, and it will be difficult to differentiate the various loops and instruments. I suggest using one drum loop, two to three percussion loops, and three to five pitched loops.

Lesson 2: Alphabet Soup *by Michael Fein*

National Standards

4. Composing and arranging music within specified guidelines

6. Listening to, analyzing, and describing music

8. Understanding relationships between music, the other arts, and disciplines outside the arts

Objectives

- Split regions, create new tracks, and drag regions

- Put the mixed-up alphabet back in order

- Spell out new words using the existing audio

Class Time Required

You should be able to complete this lesson well in a one-hour session.

Materials

- Alphabet Soup Template file located on the companion DVD

Preparations

For elementary-school students, perform the "Alphabet Song" and review the order of the alphabet.

Procedure

1. Drag the GarageBand file Alphabet Soup Template, located on the companion DVD, onto your computer's hard drive.

2. Open Alphabet Soup Template in GarageBand.

3. Press Play to listen to the file. You will hear someone reciting the alphabet backwards.

4. Press Return on your keyboard to rewind the file to the beginning.

5. Click on the audio region to select it, as shown in Figure 5.17.

Figure 5.17 Click on the audio region to select it.

Tip: A region will be a bright color when it is selected and a pale color when it is not selected.

6. Press Play and then press Stop immediately after hearing "Z."

7. Press Command+T or select Edit > Split to insert a new region boundary.

8. Continue this process for each letter (see Figure 5.18).

Figure 5.18 Split the audio region at the start of each new letter.

Tip: You can split regions quickly by pressing Command+T while the file plays. This is especially helpful when splitting regions with a reasonable amount of silence between the audio segments.

9. Click somewhere in the gray area of the Arrange window to deselect the audio regions.

10. Open the Track Editor by clicking on the Scissors icon in the bottom toolbar.

11. Double-click the name of the first region. It most likely is currently named "Alphabet Backwards.1," as shown in Figure 5.19.

Figure 5.19 Double-click the name of the first region in the Track Editor.

12. Rename the first region "Z" and press Return (see Figure 5.20).

Figure 5.20 Rename the first region "Z."

13. Continue naming each region appropriately ("Y" through "A"), as shown in Figure 5.21.

Figure 5.21 Continue naming each region appropriately.

14. To put the alphabet back in order, it would be easiest to create a new track. Create a new basic track by selecting Track > New Basic Track or by using the shortcut Shift+Command+N (see Figure 5.22).

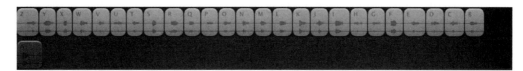

Figure 5.22 Select Track > New Basic Track.

15. Drag region A to the start of the new Basic track, as shown in Figure 5.23.

Figure 5.23 Drag region A to the start of the new Basic track.

16. Continue dragging the regions from the first track into the new Basic track until the alphabet is back in order, as shown in Figure 5.24.

Figure 5.24 Continue dragging regions until the alphabet is in the proper order.

17. Listen to the file and evaluate your edits. Does the speech flow smoothly? If not, you may need to drag the regions a bit closer together.

Tip: When dragging regions around, keep the Track Editor open to see a more detailed view.

Tip: If you accidentally cut off part of a word, use the Trim tool to bring back the missing audio. Place your cursor in the lower-right or -left corner of any region to bring up the Trim tool shown in Figure 5.25 and click and drag to reveal more audio in the region.

Figure 5.25 The Trim tool.

18. Create another new Basic track (Track > New Basic Track or use the shortcut Shift+Command +N).

19. Use this new track to spell out new words. Try spelling out a word, your name, or even an entire sentence! Be sure to Option-drag to copy regions. See Figure 5.26.

Figure 5.26   Spell out new words, such as "HELLO."

20. Export the finished project by selecting Share > Send Song to iTunes or Share > Export Song to Disk.

Extensions

Add effect plug-ins to the various tracks to modify the sound of the voice. See Chapter 3 or the lessons in Chapter 9, "Recording Your Own Audio in GarageBand," for detailed instructions on adding effect plug-ins to an Audio track.

Create a vocabulary review activity. Students or the teacher can create a file with relevant vocabulary words (possibly from a current reading activity) spelled out in new tracks. Students can then record the definitions for the various words in the appropriate tracks. For example, the teacher may spell out "A-C-O-U-S-T-I-C-S," and the students can record themselves reciting the definition ("the properties or qualities of a room or building that determine how sound is transmitted in it"). See Chapter 3 or the lessons in Chapter 9 for detailed instructions on recording new audio into GarageBand (see Figure 5.27).

Figure 5.27   Spell out a word and record the definition into a new Basic track.

6 Getting Started with MIDI in Mixcraft

This chapter contains two lessons to help you get started with MIDI in Mixcraft. Please see the companion DVD for a written tutorial for getting started with MIDI in Mixcraft, as well as a video tutorial.

Lesson 1: Pachelbel's Loops *by Richard McCready*

National Standards

3. Improvising melodies, variations, and accompaniments

4. Composing and arranging music within specified guidelines

Objectives

- Learn how to use record your own loops in Mixcraft using a MIDI keyboard.

- Learn how to arm a track, how to select instrument sounds from the provided sounds within Mixcraft, and how to record MIDI data.

- Learn how to find the Notation and Piano Roll views in Mixcraft and how to edit and quantize a loop you have recorded.

Class Time Required

You should be able to complete this lesson well in two one-hour sessions.

Materials

- Computer with Mixcraft installed.

- Internet connection.

- Headphones or monitor speakers.

- MIDI keyboard preferred (though you can use the Musical Typing option in Mixcraft if you don't have a MIDI keyboard).

- Starter file: Pachelbel Project Starter on the companion DVD.

You will find an example of a completed project on the companion DVD. Look for a file titled Pachelbel's Loops.mx5 and an MP3 file titled Pachelbel's Loops Mixdown. mp3.

Procedure

1. Navigate to the Pachelbel Project Starter.mx5 file on the companion DVD. Double-click the file name, and the file will open in Mixcraft. You will see a Mixcraft window with just one instrument loaded—a Synth Electric Bass. Click the Play button (or press the spacebar) and listen to the song. You will probably recognize it as the slow-moving bass line from Johann Pachelbel's famous "Canon in D" (although this version is in the key of C). You'll also realize that it is the same eight notes repeated (or looped) eight times—they even used loops to compose music back in the 17th century!

    Select File > Save As and save the song to your hard drive with a new name. Remember to keep saving every few minutes as you work through this project.

2. After you have listened to the song, press the Rewind to Beginning button. Turn on the metronome by selecting Mix > Metronome and then listen to the beginning of the song again. You will hear that there are four metronome clicks for every long tone in the music—all of the notes in the bass line are whole notes, so they last the length of four quarter notes. You can adjust the volume of the metronome by selecting File > Preferences and choosing the Metronome tab.

3. Select the bass line loop by clicking on its name. Now select the Sound tab in the lower part of the screen (the Details section). This is where you can see what the loop looks like in MIDI data and in notation. Two buttons at the lower left will toggle between Piano Roll view (the button has five horizontal lines) and Notation view (the button has a quarter note). Press Play again, and you can watch the notes as Mixcraft cycles through the loop. You can switch between Piano Roll view and Notation view without affecting the music.

    You can also change the tempo (or speed) of the music by selecting the Project tab in the Details section. The original speed of the music is 100 beats per minute. If you raise this number, the music will go faster; if you lower it, the music will go slower.

4. You are going to add a new melody over the bass line. Add a new Instrument track to the song by selecting Track > Insert Track > Virtual Instrument Track. Once the track has been added, you can choose a sound for it by pressing the Piano icon just to the left of the Mute button in the Instrument Name panel. Choose a category of instrument and then choose an instrument preset. If you have a MIDI keyboard, you will be able to hear what the instrument sounds like by pressing some keys on your MIDI keyboard. If you do not have a MIDI

keyboard, select Musical Typing, and you will be able to hear the instrument by pressing the appropriate keys on your computer keyboard.

Try some different instrument presets until you find a sound you like and then click on Close Window. Press Play and try improvising a melody over the bass line. Use any white notes on your MIDI keyboard (notes on the ASDF line if you're using Musical Typing) and play half notes. (This means you will play two notes in the time of one bass line note, or one note every two metronome clicks.) By using white notes only, your melody will always sound "correct" against the bass line.

5.   Press Rewind to Beginning and arm your new Instrument track by pressing Arm in the Instrument Name panel. You're going to record a segment of melody in Measures 9–16. Press the Record button, and you will hear the bass line begin to play. When it finishes its first loop, it will be at Measure 9. Record a melody for eight measures—use white notes and play just half notes.

After you've played 16 notes (one time through the bass loop), you will be at Measure 17. Stop recording and press Stop. If you're unhappy with what you just played, you can press Ctrl+Z and do another take. Try not to be a perfectionist and do too many takes—you'll just tire yourself out. After you have a recording you're happy with, press the Arm button again to disarm the track.

6.   Select the new recording by clicking its name in the Sequencer window. (Its name will be the instrument name you chose.) Select the Sound tab in the Details section and choose Piano Roll view. In the top row, select Snap Measure and then select Quantize.

In the Quantize dialog box that follows, make sure Quantize All is selected and select 1/2 Notes as the option for both Quantize Note Start and Quantize Note Length. Quantize Note Start and Quantize Note Length should be checked; Swing Amount should not be checked. Click OK, and Mixcraft will now snap your recorded notes onto the beat for you. This means that even if you weren't perfectly on the beat when you recorded your melody, you are now.

Right-click on the recorded loop in the Sequencer window directly under the number 9 and select Split. Do the same at the number 17. You should now have three regions. Delete the outer two by right-clicking on their name bars and choosing Delete. Right-click on the name bar of the remaining loop and select Make into Loop. Now duplicate that loop five times so it fills the timeline between numbers 9 and 57 (to the end of the 56th measure). Listen to your whole song so far.

7.   Add a new Instrument track and find a new sound you like. As you listen to the song, improvise a melody using white notes in quarter-note lengths. This means you will be playing a note on every metronome click. When you are ready, arm

the track and record an eight-measure loop beginning at Measure 17. You will play 32 notes in this loop and finish when the Sequencer gets to number 25. When you have a take you like, quantize it in the Sound tab's Piano Roll Editor, but this time you should select 1/4 Notes as the option for both Quantize Note Start and Quantize Note Length. Trim the loop so it lasts between the numbers 17 and 25 exactly, make it into a loop, and duplicate it three times so it fills the timeline between the numbers 17 and 49 (the end of the 48th measure).

8. Add a fourth Instrument track and find another new sound. As you listen to the song, improvise a melody using white notes in eighth-note lengths. This means you will be playing two notes in the time of each metronome click. You may find that you are struggling to keep up with the speed of the music, and you may wish you could record this new melody slower. Thankfully, that's easy when recording MIDI data. Lower the speed in the Project tab and record the notes at a slow speed. When you're happy with the recording, you can bring the project tempo back to its original speed, and it will seem to the listener that you recorded the notes at a faster speed.

When you are ready to record, arm the track and play an eight-measure loop beginning at Measure 25. You will play 64 notes in this loop and finish when the Sequencer gets to the number 33. When you have a take you like, quantize it in the Sound tab's Piano Roll Editor, but this time you should select 1/8 Notes as the option for both Quantize Note Start and Quantize Note Length. Trim the loop so it lasts between the numbers 25 and 33 exactly, make it into a loop, and duplicate it once so it fills the timeline between the numbers 25 and 41 (the end of the 40th measure).

9. When you have finished recording the last Instrument track, you should have four instruments. You can turn off the metronome before you mix the song by selecting Mix > Metronome.

10. Select the Mixer tab. As you listen to your song, use the volume faders to adjust the relative volume of each track so that each instrument is equally audible. You will notice that you can change the instrument sounds by clicking the Piano icon at the top of the channel strip or in the Instrument panel name in the Sequencer window. This is one of the great advantages of recording MIDI data. With audio recordings, you can't change the original sound, but you can with MIDI data. That way, if you decide that any of your instruments don't sound good together, you can change one (or all) of them.

Listen carefully as you mix to make sure each new sound in the music blends with the sounds that are already playing. This means any new sound should be audible but not masking the other sounds. Use the L-R sliders above the volume faders to adjust where your instruments are from left to right in the mix. Imagine where you would like them to be on stage as they would be in live performance and reflect this by mixing them to the appropriate side in the mix. You can adjust the Hi, Mid, and Lo responses in each track by turning the knobs in the EQ section of the Mixer. As you mix, make sure that the volume levels do not light up the red warning light at the top of the volume faders.

11. Select Track > Show Master Track. Add a reverb unit to the Global Effects for the Master Track. Choose an appropriate reverb preset for your music. You may like to make your music sound as if it is being performed in a big church or a concert hall. Listen to the music again and check to make sure the Master Track volume level does not peak into the red. When you are satisfied that your song is the best that it can be, mix it down to an MP3 using File > Mix Down To > MP3. Make sure to play your song for friends or family members to see whether they like it.

Extensions

Listen to a recording or a live performance of Pachelbel's "Canon in D" and see whether you can hear the repeating bass line throughout. You can also try listening to some other music that uses the same (or a similar) bass line. Examples are "Pachelbel's Frolics" by Eileen Ivers, found on her self-titled *Eileen Ivers* album, or "Go West" by the Pet Shop Boys, found on their *PopArt: The Hits* compilation. "Go West" was originally recorded by the Village People, but the Pet Shop Boys' recording is a good one for listening, as it was made using MIDI sequencers. You should also look ahead to Chapter 17 for ways to put your song online so other people can listen to it.

Lesson 2: That 1970s Thing *by Richard McCready*

National Standards

3. Improvising melodies, variations, and accompaniments

4. Composing and arranging music within specified guidelines

5. Reading and notating music

Objectives

- Learn how to add and delete Virtual Instrument tracks in Mixcraft.

- Learn how to record MIDI parts in different takes and merge them into one MIDI clip.

- Learn how to quantize (tidy) notes visually, how to edit note velocities, and how to record drum sounds using a MIDI keyboard.

- Learn how to add effects to individual tracks during mixdown.

Class Time Required

You should be able to complete this lesson well in two one-hour sessions.

Materials

- Computer with Mixcraft installed

- Internet connection

- Headphones or monitor speakers

- MIDI keyboard preferred (though you can use the Musical Typing option in Mixcraft if you don't have a MIDI keyboard)

You will find an example of a completed project on the companion DVD. Look for a file titled That 1970s Thing.mx5 and an MP3 file titled That 1970s Thing Mixdown .mp3.

Procedure

1. Launch Mixcraft and select the third option (Build Virtual Instrument Tracks) from the New Project screen. You will see that you are given a template with two Instrument tracks and six Audio tracks. You do not need the Audio tracks for this project, so delete them. Select each one individually and click Track > Delete Track. It's easier if you scroll down to the last track in the Sequencer and delete them from the bottom up. Add two Virtual Instrument tracks by selecting Track > Add Track > Virtual Instrument Track (or use the shortcut key

combination Ctrl+E) twice. Save your work so far. Remember to keep saving every few minutes as you work through this project.

2. Choose a piano sound for the first track. Click on the Piano icon in the Instrument Name panel (which reads "1 Instrument Track"), choose either the Acoustic Piano or the Electric Piano category, and find a sound you like. Remember, you can audition the sounds by playing your MIDI keyboard (or using Musical Typing) when you highlight an instrument preset.

3. Enable the metronome by selecting Mix > Metronome. You will need a couple of count-in measures to know when to record, so enable this option in the Metronome tab under File > Preferences.

4. Arm Track 1 (click the Arm button in the panel by the instrument name) and click Record on the transport. You will hear two measures (eight beats) of count-in. After the eighth beat, record the 16 notes shown in Figure 6.1 (one on each beat) and then click Stop.

Figure 6.1 Notes to record in Step 4.

5. Click Rewind to Beginning and click Play to listen to what you just recorded. If you are unhappy with that take, press Ctrl+Z to erase it, and you can record it again. If the metronome speed was too fast for you, slow it down in the Project Details section. (You can bring it back to 120 bpm later.)

6. When you are happy with the take, click Rewind to Beginning again and click Record. The track is already armed, so you'll be able to record the next 16 notes, shown in Figure 6.2, over what you've already recorded. You'll hear the metronome and your previous recording in the headphones. When you listen back to what you've recorded, you'll now hear both sets of notes together. Don't worry if they're not quite in time—we'll fix that later. If you need to go back and re-record the last set of notes, you can press Ctrl+Z to undo your latest take without losing the first set of notes you recorded earlier.

Figure 6.2 Notes to record in Step 6.

7. Use the same process to record the third set of notes, shown in Figure 6.3. When you are happy with your recording, click Arm to disarm the track.

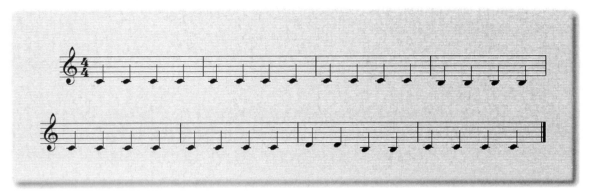

Figure 6.3 Notes to record in Step 7.

8. The takes you made are now stacked on top of one another on Track 1, and you will only be able to see the most recent one on top. Select the topmost region by selecting its name bar. Then select all the regions underneath it by choosing Edit > Select All or by using the shortcut key combination Ctrl+A. Now select Edit > Merge to New Clip or use the shortcut key combination Ctrl+W to merge all the regions into one clip.

9. Select the Sound tab in the Project Details section. In the Notation Editor, you will be able to see the notes you recorded as three-note chords. Press Tidy Notes > 1/4 Note above the Notation view to visually quantize your notes. In the Piano Roll Editor, quantize the notes using 1/4 notes for Quantize Note Start and 1/8 notes for Quantize Note Length. Now when you flip back to the Notation Editor, you'll see your notes are still represented by quarter notes (which is how you would read them); but when you listen, they are eighth notes with eighth-note rests in between. This sounds more like piano stabs, which is the sound we want for the piano part in this project.

Return to the Piano Roll Editor and observe how there is a vertical line underneath every note. This represents the velocity of each note—that is, how hard you pressed the key on the keyboard. As you hover over the lines, your cursor will change to a pencil. You can use the pencil to alter the height of each vertical line so you can even out the velocity of the notes you played. One great feature of Mixcraft is that you can hold the pencil and drag across the tops of the vertical lines to align them. It takes some getting used to, and you may have to go back and edit some parts again, but it's a very handy way to even out the velocities quickly.

10. Select the second track and find a bass sound for it. Arm the track and record the 16 bass notes shown in Figure 6.4. When you are happy with your recording, disarm the track and tidy the notes in the Notation Editor using Tidy Notes > 1/4 Note. Quantize them in the Piano Roll Editor of the Sound tab using 1/4 notes for Quantize Note Start and 1/8 notes for Quantize Note Length. Even out the velocities by drawing across the vertical lines underneath the notes.

Figure 6.4 Notes to record in Step 10.

11. In the third Instrument track, click the Piano icon and select a drum kit from the Drums category (but not the KIT – SFX Kit preset). Make sure you scroll down to the presets, which begin with the word KIT. Now when you press the notes on your MIDI keyboard or use Musical Typing, you'll hear different drums on each note. Find the bass drum sound and the snare sound. These are usually on the C and C# one octave below middle C. These are sometimes called C3 and C#3. If you have a 25-note keyboard (or are using Musical Typing), you will need to press the Octave Down button on your keyboard. Then you will find the bass and snare sounds as the lowest two notes.

12. Arm Track 3 (the drum track) and record 16 bass drum sounds, one on each beat. Then go back and record the snare drum sound on every alternating beat (the even beats 2, 4, and so on). When you are happy with your recording, disarm the track. Select everything in Track 3 and merge the sounds to a new

clip using Edit > Merge to New Clip. Tidy the notes as 1/4 notes in the Notation Editor and then quantize them to 1/4 notes in the Piano Roll Editor.

Note that it doesn't matter whether you select the quantize length as 1/4 notes or 1/8 notes or even 1/16 or 1/32 notes—drum sounds don't have length, so it only matters that the start of the note (the moment the drum is hit) is on the correct beat. You should, however, even out the velocities of the notes.

13. Listen to everything you've created so far. You now have a 1970s-style rhythm track ready for you to create a guitar solo. Add a guitar sound to Track 4. Arm the track and try a few takes, improvising a guitar solo over the top of the rhythm track. Use just the white notes on the keyboard to be safe, though if you're feeling adventurous you can add some "blue notes"—Eb and Bb. They're not actually colored blue—they are just used often as extra scale notes in the blues so we call them *blue notes*. Blues and rock guitarists play them a lot when they improvise a solo.

    When you have a take you like, disarm the track. Do not quantize this track or even out the velocities—it'll sound much better to leave it just the way you recorded it.

14. Tidy the end of your tracks by trimming them at the end of Measure 8 (number 9 on the timeline) and deleting the extra at the end. There shouldn't be any notes there—that was just what was left before you hit Stop every time you recorded. If you previously brought your project tempo down for recording, return it to 120 bpm in the Project Details tab. Enable loop play by clicking the curly arrow near the time code in the center of the screen or using Mix > Loop Playback Mode. Disable the metronome by clicking Mix > Metronome.

15. Select the Mixer tab. As you listen to your song, use the volume faders to adjust the relative volume of each track so that each instrument is equally audible. Use the L-R sliders above the volume faders to adjust where your instruments are from left to right in the mix. Imagine where you would like them to be on stage as they would be in live performance, and reflect this by mixing them to the appropriate side in the mix.

    You can adjust the Hi, Mid, and Lo responses in each track by turning the knobs in the EQ section of the Mixer. As you mix, make sure that the volume levels do not light up the red warning light at the top of the volume faders.

16. Click the FX button at the top of the Piano track. Add the Acoustica Compressor to the Global Effects menu. Choose a good preset to give your piano sound some punch. Add a different Acoustica Compressor preset to each of the other tracks by using the FX button at the top of each channel strip. Each track now has its own Compressor unit—they are not sharing the same one!

You can also add some guitar effects to your Guitar track by selecting Acoustica Delay, Flanger, Chorus, Distortion, and so on. This will help thicken and define your sound, but don't go overboard or you'll end up with an ugly guitar sound instead. Keep checking to make sure your volume faders do not go into the red zone. The compressors may in fact give you room to boost your faders a little.

17. Add the Acoustica Reverb unit to the FX for the master fader. Choose an appropriate reverb preset for your music. You may like to make your music sound as if it is being performed in a canyon or a gymnasium. Listen to the music again and check that the Master Track volume level does not peak into the red. When you are satisfied that your song is the best that it can be, mix it down to an MP3 using File > Mix Down To > MP3. Make sure to play your song for friends or family members to see whether they like it.

Extensions

Find other drum sounds on the drum kit you used in Track 3. Add some more drum sounds to the recording and merge them into that track to make your music more exciting. Some drum fills and cymbals might work well. You can also try making up your own chord progression to record for the piano line and bass line in this project. You should also look ahead to Chapter 17 for ways to put your song online so other people can listen to it.

7 Getting Started with MIDI in GarageBand

This chapter contains two lessons to help you get started with MIDI in GarageBand. Please see the companion DVD for a written tutorial for getting started with MIDI in GarageBand. The companion DVD also includes a video tutorial to help you with this chapter.

Lesson 1: Chord Bank Composition *by Michael Fein*

National Standards

2. Performing on instruments, alone and with others, a varied repertoire of music

3. Improvising melodies, variations, and accompaniments

4. Composing and arranging music within specified guidelines

5. Reading and notating music

6. Listening to, analyzing, and describing music

7. Evaluating music and music performances

Objectives

- Compose a chord progression using a bank of prerecorded chords.

- Compose a melody by moving the notes of the given melody to fit the chord progression using only chord tones.

- Compose a bass line using the root and 5th of each chord.

- Improvise a percussion accompaniment.

Class Time Required

You should be able to complete this lesson well in three one-hour sessions.

Materials

- Chord Bank Composition Template file located on the companion DVD

Preparations

1. Direct students to www.musictheory.net. This site has an outstanding series of lessons that cover beginning to advanced music theory concepts. Students should watch the lesson entitled Common Chord Progressions.

2. Play the following musical game with the class to help the students begin to identify the sound of various progressions. Select one student to write a chord on the board. (The teacher will play the chord.) That student will pass the chalkboard or white-board marker to another student, and that student will write a different chord that typically follows the first chord. Continue this activity until all of the students have written a chord on the board. Perform the entire progression on a piano/keyboard. See Figure 7.1.

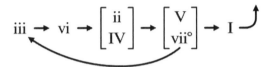

Figure 7.1 Chord progression chart.

Procedure

1. Drag the GarageBand file Chord Bank Composition Template, located on the companion DVD, onto your computer's hard drive.

2. Open Chord Bank Composition Template in GarageBand.

3. Solo the Chord Bank track by clicking the Headphone icon under the track name (see Figure 7.2). When a track is soloed, the headphones will light up yellow.

Figure 7.2 The Headphone/Solo icon.

4. Play the file. You will hear the diatonic chords based on the C Major scale.

5. Using the chord progression chart, compose a chord progression on paper. I strongly suggest using paper and pencil before you try to create the chord progression in GarageBand!

   - You may use one or two chords per bar. Try to use a mix of one or two chords per bar to keep the harmonic rhythm interesting. The harmonic rhythm is simply the rhythm of the chords. If you had only one chord per bar for every bar, that would be a very boring harmonic rhythm. Similarly, if you had two chords per bar for every bar, that would also be a boring harmonic rhythm.

- You should start and end the progression on I (C Major).
- This chord progression must last eight measures.

6. Drag the various chords from the Chord Bank track to the Chord Progression track to compose your chord progression in GarageBand. If you used chords more than once, you can copy them by holding the Option key and clicking and dragging the region. If you are using two chords in a single bar, shorten each region so it only lasts two beats by using the Trim tool. (Note: Place your cursor in the lower-right corner of a region to reveal the Trim tool.) See Figure 7.3.

Figure 7.3 Compose a chord progression using chords from the Chord Bank track.

7. Listen to the chord progression. Are there any chords that sound out of place? Is the harmonic rhythm interesting? Make any modifications to your chord progression at this time, because the melody and bass parts are based on the chord progression.

8. Unsolo the Chord Progression track and solo the Melody track.

9. Play the file. You will hear a melody that plays an interesting rhythm but stays only on the pitch C.

10. Click on the region located in the Melody track.

11. Open the Track Editor. The default view shows you a piano roll version of the notes with a piano keyboard stretched along the left side of the window. You can also view the traditional music notation by clicking on the Score button. See Figure 7.4.

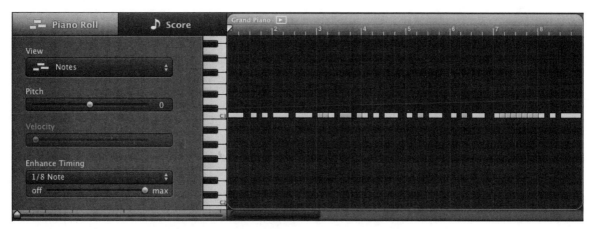

Figure 7.4 Piano Roll view of the Melody track.

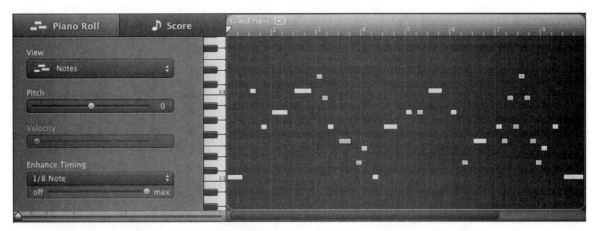

Figure 7.5 Drag each note up or down to a chord tone in each bar.

12. Drag each note up or down to a chord tone in each bar. Do not use any non-chord tones. See Figure 7.5.

Note: A chord tone is a note within a given chord. For example, if the sounding chord is C Major (I), the chord tones are C-E-G. You may use any C, E, or G in any octave while the C Major (I) chord is sounding.

Tip: If you drag notes up or down in the Piano Roll view in the Track Editor, a help tag will appear that indicates the note name.

---

13. Solo the chord progression so both the Chord Progression and the Melody track are soloed.

14. Listen to the melody along with the chord progression. Do any melody notes sound dissonant? If so, you may have accidentally used a non-chord tone.

15. Unsolo both the Chord Progression and the Melody track and solo the Bass track.

16. Play the file. Similar to the original melody region, you will hear a bass part that plays an interesting rhythm but stays only on the pitch C.

17. Click on the region located in the Bass track and open the Track Editor. See Figure 7.6.

18. Drag each note up or down to either the root or the 5th of the chord for each bar. For example, if the sounding chord is C Major (I), the bass notes available are C (the root) and G (the 5th). Typically, you will play the root on the first note of the sounding chord. See Figure 7.7.

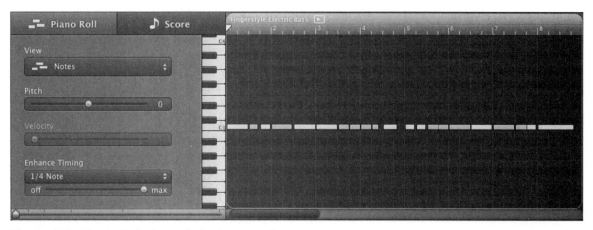

Figure 7.6   Piano Roll view of the Bass track.

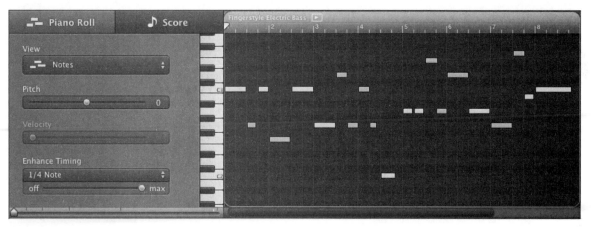

Figure 7.7   Drag each note up or down to the root or 5th of the sounding chord.

19.   Unsolo the Bass track and listen to the melody, bass, and chord progression all together. Do any bass notes sound dissonant? If so, you may have used a bass note that was not the root or 5th of the sounding chord.

Currently, all of the instruments sounds are Grand Piano. Although there is nothing wrong with a piano trio, you can add a lot of interest to your composition by using a variety of instrument sounds.

20.   Open the Track Info pane by clicking on the "i" icon in the toolbar, as shown in Figure 7.8.

Figure 7.8   Track Info icon.

21.   Click on the Chord Progression track and play the file.

22.   As the file plays, click on a new instrument category and then a new instrument in the Track Info pane. You should hear the sound of your chord progression change.

Tip: You can add many more instrument sounds to GarageBand by purchasing GarageBand JamPacks. Most JamPacks cost about $99 and include both loops and software instruments. You can also try searching the Internet for additional GarageBand software instruments. I recommend downloading the GarageBand instrument packs created by Ben Boldt. (Search "GarageBand Boldt.") The Boldt instrument packs are shareware, which means they are free to download, install, and use, and you can choose to pay a small fee to the creator.

---

23. Repeat Steps 21 and 22 with the Melody and Bass tracks to create an interesting instrumental ensemble. See Figure 7.9.

Figure 7.9 Select new software instruments for each track.

24. You are now going to create a percussion accompaniment track. Create a new track by selecting Track > New Track or using the shortcut Option+Command +N (see Figure 7.10).

Figure 7.10 Select Track > New Track.

25. Select Software Instrument in the next window, as shown in Figure 7.11.

Figure 7.11 Select Software Instrument.

26. In the Track Info pane, select Drum Kits and then select a drum kit.

27. Test the sound by pressing on your MIDI keyboard or by using the Musical Typing keyboard (Window > Musical Typing).

28. Pick one note on your keyboard, such as snare drum. The snare drum sound is located on the fourth lowest D or E on the Musical Typing keyboard and on the lowest D or E on most MIDI keyboards. You may need to try various octaves or pitches to find a drum/percussion sound you think will work well with your other instruments.

29. Click the red Record button on the toolbar, shown in Figure 7.12, and improvise a drum accompaniment.

Figure 7.12   The Record button.

30. To improve the rhythmic accuracy of your percussion part, you can quantize your notes so they fit exactly on a given rhythmic value. Click on Enhance Timing in the Track Editor. Notice the variety of rhythmic values available. Select the *smallest* rhythmic value that you just performed. For most recordings you will likely use 1/16 or 1/8; however, you may also use the triplet values if you played any triplet rhythms during your improvisation. See Figure 7.13.

Figure 7.13   The Enhance Timing portion of the Track Editor.

31. Listen to the entire file and focus on the volume of each track. Adjust the gain (a.k.a. volume) slider in each track so the sound of each track blends with the others. A single instrument should not stand out.

32. Listen again and focus on the panning of each track. *Panning* refers to the placement of the sound in the left/right stereo field. If you go to see a concert, some musicians are on the right side of the stage, some are on the left, and some are in the center. The panning of your composition should reflect this reality. For example, try panning the chords to the left, the melody to the right, the bass slightly to the right, and the drum improvisation slightly to the left. Try to balance the right and left sides. It would sound odd if a majority of the sound came from just the left side or just the right side. See Figure 7.14.

33. Evaluate your composition. Did you:
    - Compose a chord progression that fits the common chord progression chart?
    - Correctly use chord tones only throughout the melody?
    - Correctly use root/5th in the bass part?

Panning   Volume
knobs   sliders

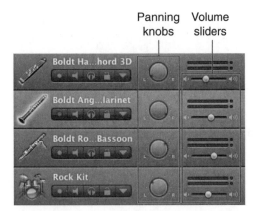

Figure 7.14 Adjust the volume and panning of each track to create a nice blend and an interesting stereo image.

- Assign new instruments to each track?
- Improvise a drum/percussion accompaniment and quantize the recording?
- Adjust the volume/panning of each track so all the instruments blend together nicely?

34. Export the finished project by selecting Share > Send Song to iTunes or Share > Export Song to Disk.

Extensions

Add additional drum/percussion improvisation tracks. Be sure to quantize after each recording by using the Enhance Timing pop-up window in the Track Editor.

Compose a B section by creating a new chord progression using the chord bank. Because the B section should be a contrast to the A section, you do not need to start and end on I (C Major). It would actually be very normal to begin the B section on F Major (IV) or A minor (vi).

Compose a new melody for your B section. Record a rhythm using only pitch C and be sure to quantize the recording. Then, based on your B section chord progression, drag the melody notes to chord tones in the Track Editor.

Compose a new bass line for your B section. Record a rhythm using only pitch C and be sure to quantize the recording. Then, based on your B section chord progression, drag the bass notes to root/5th in the Track Editor.

Lesson 2: Mozart Minuet Composition *by Michael Fein*

National Standards

2. Performing on instruments, alone and with others, a varied repertoire of music

3. Improvising melodies, variations, and accompaniments

4. Composing and arranging music within specified guidelines

5. Reading and notating music

6. Listening to, analyzing, and describing music

7. Evaluating music and music performances

Objectives

- Create a new GarageBand project, set the time signature appropriately, and import a MIDI file.

- Arrange MIDI regions to compose a new version of the Mozart Minuet.

- Improvise a bass line for the minuet using a MIDI keyboard.

- Improvise a rhythmic accompaniment using a MIDI keyboard.

- Print and perform the final composition.

Class Time Required

You should be able to complete this lesson well in two one-hour sessions.

Materials

- Mozart Minuet.mid file located on the companion DVD

Preparations

1. Use a music dictionary to define the word "minuet." You may also use an online music dictionary, such as the one located at www.music.vt.edu/musicdictionary or www.naxos.com/education/glossary.asp.

2. Listen to a variety of Mozart minuets. Using the iTunes Music Store, search for "Mozart Minuet" and listen to the preview clips of available songs.

Procedure

1. Drag the file Mozart Minuet.mid from the companion DVD to your desktop to copy the file onto your computer's hard drive.

2. Launch GarageBand.

3. Create a new GarageBand project by selecting File > New or using the shortcut Command+N (see Figure 7.15).

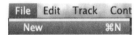

Figure 7.15 Select File > New.

4. Select New Project in the left pane of the QuickStart window and then select Piano from the list of icons (see Figure 7.16).

Figure 7.16 In the QuickStart window, select New Project and the Piano template.

5. Name the file Mozart Minuet Composition. Be sure to set the time signature to 3/4 because a minuet is in 3/4 meter (see Figure 7.17). Save the file to your desktop.

Figure 7.17 Select 3/4 for the time signature.

6. Delete the first track named Grand Piano by pressing Command+Delete.

7. Click on the Finder icon in your Dock and navigate to the desktop.

8. Drag Mozart Minuet.mid from the Finder window into the gray area in your new GarageBand project. This will import the MIDI file (see Figure 7.18).

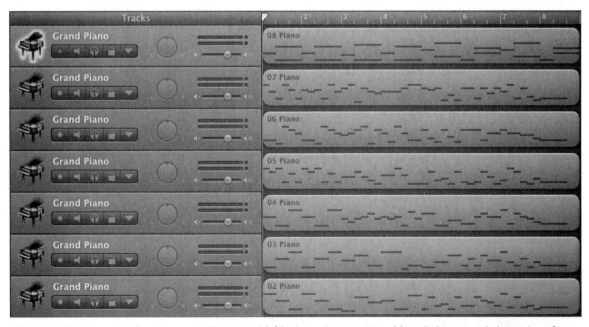

Figure 7.18 Import the Mozart Minuet.mid file into GarageBand by clicking and dragging from the Finder.

9.   Solo one track at a time and listen to each track individually. The top track of this MIDI file is the harmony track. The six tracks below will be used to create an original melody for your minuet. The six melodic tracks can be used interchangeably. This means that Bar 1 from any track will work with Bar 2 of any track and so forth.

10. Select the six bottom melodic tracks.

11. Place the play head at Bar 2 and press Command+T to split all of the regions at Bar 2.

12. Continue splitting the melodic tracks at Bars 3, 4, 5, 6, 7, and 8 (see Figure 7.19).

Figure 7.19 Split the six bottom melodic tracks at the start of each bar.

13. Click in the gray area of the Arrange window to deselect the regions.

14. Create a new Software Instrument track. (Choose Track > New or use the shortcut Option+Command+N and select Software Instrument.) You will use this track to compose your melody.

15. Mute all six of the melodic tracks by clicking the Speaker icon in each track. The Speaker icon will light up blue when a track is muted.

16. Drag one of the regions for Bar 1 from any of the melodic tracks into the top track.

17. Play the file and evaluate the sound of the melodic region that you chose and how it works with the harmony track. Try out another region by moving a different region for Bar 1 into the top track.

Figure 7.20 Drag one region for each measure into a new Software Instrument track to compose a complete eight-bar melody.

18. Continue using regions from each bar to compose a complete eight-bar minuet melody (see Figure 7.20).

19. Select all of the regions in your top melody track and join them together by choosing Edit > Join or using the shortcut Command+J (see Figures 7.21 and 7.22).

Figure 7.21 The new melody *before* joining.

Figure 7.22 The new melody *after* joining.

20. Select the melody track and select a new instrument sound from the Track Info pane. You certainly can keep the Grand Piano sound, but it may be more interesting to use a different sound.

21. Create a new Software Instrument. (Choose Track > New or use the shortcut Option+Command+N and select Software Instrument.)

22. This new track will serve as the bass part for the minuet, so I recommend selecting a bass instrument sound from the Track Info pane. If you decide to select a different instrument category, be sure to play the instrument relatively low on the MIDI keyboard so it serves the sonic purpose of a bass.

   The chord progression for this song is C | C | G7 | C | D | G | D | G.

23. Select Control > Count In, as shown in Figure 7.23. This will provide you with a one-bar count-in before you begin recording.

Figure 7.23 Select Control > Count In.

24. Record an improvised bass line using only the roots of the chords listed a moment ago.

25. Quantize your bass recording to the lowest rhythmic value that you performed in the previous step (see Figure 7.24). Most likely, you will quantize to the 1/4 note or 1/8 note.

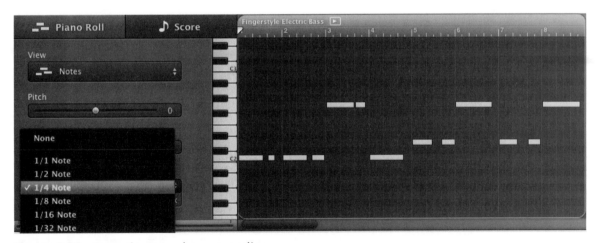

Figure 7.24 Quantize your bass recording.

26. Create another new Software Instrument track.

27. Select a sound from the Drum Kits category in the Track Info pane.

28. Record an improvised drum/percussion accompaniment track using a single drum sound.

29. Add in additional drum/percussion tracks as you see fit (see Figure 7.25).

30. Adjust the panning and volume of the various tracks to create an interesting mix. Adjust the volumes of each track so they all blend together well. Adjust the

Figure 7.25 Record one or more improvised drum/percussion tracks.

panning of each track so some tracks are more on the left side and others are more on the right side, but remember to balance the left and right channels.

Tip: If a track will not allow you to adjust volume or panning, open the Automation window for that track by clicking on the down arrow below the track name (see Figure 7.26). Then turn off track automation by clicking the green square next to Track Volume (see Figure 7.27). **GarageBand '11 users note:** The Automation icon is now located in the lower-right corner of the track display.

Figure 7.26 Click the down arrow below the track name to open the Automation window.

Figure 7.27 Click the green square to turn off track automation.

31. Select the melody region and view it in Score view in the Track Editor (see Figure 7.28).

Figure 7.28 View the melody region in Score view.

32. Print this part by selecting File > Print or pressing Command+P (see Figure 7.29).

Figure 7.29 Select File > Print to print the melody part.

33. Print the remaining parts (harmony, improvised bass, and all improvised drum/ percussion parts).

Tip: If the notation printout is too low for a given instrument, transpose the region by dragging the Pitch slider in the Track Info pane. Try transposing −24, −12, +12, or +24 to make the music playable by the given instrument.

Tip: If the instrument that will perform the part is a transposing instrument, you will need to transpose the pitch of the given region. For B♭ instruments, such as trumpet, tenor/soprano saxophone, and clarinet, transpose the region −10, +2, or +14. For E♭ instruments, such as alto/baritone saxophone, transpose the region −3 or +9. Note that this tip is for printout purposes only!

---

34. Perform the piece with one student on each part.

Extensions

Create a repeat with dynamic contrast. Loop the regions so the eight-bar phrase occurs three times. Select Track > Show Master Track. Reduce the volume in the middle repetition by clicking nodes on the line in the Master Track (this track is likely displaying the name Master Volume) and dragging the volume down. Bring the volume back to 0.0 dB for the final repeat. See Figure 7.30.

Figure 7.30 Reduce the volume of the Master Track during the middle repetition.

Many minuets have a contrasting section called a *trio*. Compose a trio section for your minuet. Refer to the Chord Bank Composition project for ideas on composing a new chord progression and developing a melody and bass part for the trio.

8 Recording Your Own Audio in Mixcraft

This chapter contains two lessons to help you record audio in Mixcraft. Please see the companion DVD for a written tutorial on recording audio in Mixcraft, as well as a video tutorial.

Lesson 1: Alice's Adventures in Mixcraft
by Richard McCready

National Standards

3. Improvising melodies, variations, and accompaniments

4. Composing and arranging music within specified guidelines

8. Understanding relationships between music, the other arts, and disciplines outside the arts

Objectives

- Record a passage of *Alice's Adventures in Wonderland* by Lewis Carroll and make it into a selection you might hear on an audio-book recording.

- Learn how to record using a microphone and an audio interface.

- Learn how to automate volume controls to create fades.

Class Time Required

You should be able to complete this lesson well in two one-hour sessions.

Materials

- Computer with Mixcraft installed

- Headphones

- Microphone

- Audio interface

- An acoustic musical instrument (or a friend who has one)

You will find an example of a completed project on the companion DVD. Look for a file titled Alice's Adventures in Mixcraft.mx5 and an MP3 file titled Alice's Adventures in Mixcraft Mixdown.mp3.

Procedure

1. Launch Mixcraft and select the first option (Record Yourself or Your Band) from the New Project screen. You will see that you are given a template with eight Audio tracks. You only need two Audio tracks for this project, so you can delete the others. Select each one individually and click Track > Delete Track. It's easier if you scroll down to the last track in the Sequencer and delete them from the bottom up.

   You will also notice that Mixcraft gives you a time code in minutes and seconds rather than in bars and beats. If your timeline is in bars and beats, change it to minutes and seconds by clicking the Time button, which you'll find above the fader for the first track. Save your work so far. Remember to keep saving every few minutes as you work through this project.

2. You will be recording through a microphone, so make sure your speakers are off, or you might inadvertently pick up the sound of the speakers while you're recording and create a feedback loop. You should use headphones to listen as you record this project.

   Attach your microphone to the input of your audio interface. Check the Sound Device tab of the File > Preferences screen to make sure that your audio interface is selected. In the title bar of the first track, click the down arrow to the right of the Arm button to make sure the correct channel is selected for your audio interface. Select Monitor Incoming Audio if you need to hear what you are recording through the headphones. This may cause some unfortunate delay between what you say into the microphone and what you hear, so it is probably best to leave the Monitor Incoming Audio option unchecked.

3. Arm Track 1. Speak into the microphone to make sure you are getting a strong signal. Watch the volume readout in the first track to make sure the computer is able to hear you well. If you are getting a very weak signal, you may need to turn up the gain on the microphone input on your audio interface. If your signal is too strong, you may have to lower the level.

   Be aware that your proximity to the microphone is also a contributing factor to the strength of your sound. The microphone should be just a couple of inches from your mouth as you are speaking into it. Please note that is it never right to bang a microphone to see whether it's working. You can easily damage the microphone, headphones, speakers, and even your own hearing in this way.

4.   Press the Record button and read the following passage from Lewis Carroll's *Alice's Adventures in Wonderland*. Make sure you include the title of the passage, and try to get through the whole excerpt in one take. If you make a mistake, don't worry. Just press Stop and then Rewind to Beginning and click Edit > Undo or use the shortcut key combination Ctrl+Z to undo the last recording and record again. You will learn about editing multiple takes in the next lesson.

Alice's Adventures in Wonderland **by Lewis Carroll**
Chapter 7, "A Mad Tea-Party"
There was a table set out under a tree in front of the house, and the March Hare and the Hatter were having tea at it. A Dormouse was sitting between them, fast asleep.

The table was a large one, but the three were all crowded together at one corner of it: "No room! No room!" they cried out when they saw Alice coming. "There's plenty of room!" said Alice indignantly, and she sat down in a large arm-chair at one end of the table.

The Hatter opened his eyes very wide on hearing this; but all he said was, "Why is a raven like a writing-desk?"

"I'm glad they've begun asking riddles. I believe I can guess that," Alice added aloud.

"Do you mean that you think you can find out the answer to it?" said the March Hare.

"Exactly so," said Alice.

"Then you should say what you mean," the March Hare went on.

"I do," Alice hastily replied; "at least, at least I mean what I say—that's the same thing, you know."

"You might just as well say," added the Dormouse, who seemed to be talking in his sleep, "that *I breathe when I sleep* is the same thing as *I sleep when I breathe!*"

"It is the same thing with you," said the Hatter, and he poured a little hot tea upon its nose.

The Dormouse shook its head impatiently, and said, without opening its eyes, "Of course, of course; just what I was going to remark myself."

"Have you guessed the riddle yet?" the Hatter said, turning to Alice again.

"No, I give it up," Alice replied: "what's the answer?"

"I haven't the slightest idea," said the Hatter.

"Nor I," said the March Hare.

Alice gave a weary sigh. "I think you might do something better with the time," she said, "than wasting it in asking riddles that have no answers."

---

5.   Disarm the track. Press Rewind to Beginning and listen to what you have recorded. Click on the FX button beside the Arm button and add some effects to the channel. You might like to add in a compressor to smooth out the sound or perhaps a reverb. You might also like to add in the Acoustica EQ, which will give you more control over the EQ settings of your voice than the simple EQ in Mixcraft's Mixer tab.

6.   You can trim the beginning and end of your recording by resizing the clip. Hold your mouse over the beginning of the clip, near the top, until it looks like a double-headed arrow. Click and hold, and then you can drag the start of the clip left or right. Try to line up the beginning of your clip with the moment your voice starts to read. Trim the end of the clip the same way. You can then move the clip closer to the beginning of the track by dragging its name bar. Leave a second or two at the beginning.

7.   Listen to the start of the track and make note of when your recording gets to the end of reading the title of the book and chapter. You will need to add some background music to last from the beginning up to this point. Compose or improvise some music on an acoustic instrument, or you could have a friend compose or improvise something. You can try composing or improvising along to the track to get a feel for how much music you'll need.

8.   Make sure the channel settings are correct for Track 2. Arm Track 2 and play your acoustic instrument into the microphone. You may need to get a stand to hold the microphone or have a friend hold it in place for you. Make sure you're getting a good signal. When everything is ready, you should press Rewind to Beginning and then Record. Try to record in one take, but if you need a do-over, press Stop and Rewind to Beginning again and use Edit > Undo or Ctrl+Z to undo the last recording. Disarm the track when you have finished recording.

9.   Add some FX to the track. If you used reverb on Track 1, you should probably use the same reverb on Track 2, so it sounds as if the voice and the acoustic instrument were in the same place when they were recorded.

10.   Select the newly recorded passage by clicking on its name and then copy it to the end of the track. Select Edit > Copy or press Ctrl+C, scroll to the end of the track, click somewhere in Track 2 near the point at which the voice recording finishes, and select Edit > Paste or press Ctrl+V. Listen to the end of the recording and move the music clip to a good place, so it starts just as the reading ends.

11.   Press the Toggle Automation button to the left of the FX button in Track 2. The Toggle Automation looks like a tiny line graph, and it will allow you to add some automation to the volume levels in the track. Find a point at which you would like the music in Track 2 to begin to fade and click on the horizontal line

you see going through Track 2. Click again at the point at which you would like the fade to end, hold the mouse button, and drag the point down. You will see you have created points on the line, and you now have a descending line between two of those points. This will fade out the music, just like you would do if you brought the fader in the Mixer tab down. Scroll to the end of the track and create a fade-in for the music and a fade-out for the music.

12. Listen to your work and check the levels of the voice and the music. The voice should always be audible, even when the music is playing. You can edit the level of each, either in the automation lane or by using the Mixer tab. You can also pan your voice and instrument slightly left and right—separating them slightly on either side of center is a good idea. Make sure nothing peaks into the red. (This should be second nature to you by now.) When you are satisfied that your recording is the best that it can be, mix it down to an MP3 using File > Mix Down To > MP3. Make sure to play your recording of *Alice's Adventures in Wonderland* for friends or family members to see whether they like it.

Extensions

The passage used for this unit was taken from an abridged edition of *Alice's Adventures in Wonderland*. Find an unabridged copy of the text, either in the library or on the Internet, and find a longer passage you can record. You could even try recording the whole of Chapter 7, "A Mad Tea-Party." As you record longer passages, you will need to use more background music. Select significant breaking points in the text to include some more music. You might add music where there are changes of scene, changes of character, changes of mood, and so on. Look ahead to Chapter 17, "Putting It All Together," to find ways in which you can publish your audio-book excerpt online.

Lesson 2: The Tongue Twister Tournament
by Richard McCready

National Standards

3. Improvising melodies, variations, and accompaniments

4. Composing and arranging music within specified guidelines

8. Understanding relationships between music, the other arts, and disciplines outside the arts

Objectives

■ Record a passage from a news show.

■ Add music to introduce and finish the broadcast excerpt.

■ Record a passage in segments, trim them, and join them together.

Class Time Required

You should be able to complete this lesson well in two one-hour sessions.

Materials

■ Computer with Mixcraft installed

■ Headphones

■ Microphone

■ Audio interface

■ MIDI keyboard

You will find an example of a completed project on the companion DVD. Look for a file titled The Tongue Twister Tournament and an MP3 file titled The Tongue Twister Tournament Mixdown.

Procedure

These first steps are almost the same as the early steps in the previous project, "Alice's Adventures in Mixcraft." It may seem as if you've done all this before (because you have), but it's important that you set up a session appropriately every time you get ready to record audio. You can save yourself many hours in the music studio or the broadcast studio by using proper preproduction preparation.

1. Launch Mixcraft and select the first option (Record Yourself or Your Band) from the New Project screen. You will see that you are given a template with eight Audio tracks. You only need one Audio track for this project, so delete the others. Select each one individually and click Track > Delete Track. It's easier if

you scroll down to the last track in the Sequencer and delete the tracks from the bottom up. Add one Virtual Instrument track by selecting Track > Add Track > Virtual Instrument Track or by using the shortcut key combination Ctrl+E. If your timeline is in bars and beats, change it to minutes and seconds by clicking the Time button, which you'll find above the fader for the first track. Save your work so far. Remember to keep saving every few minutes as you work through this project.

2. You will be recording through a microphone, so make sure your speakers are off, or you might inadvertently pick up the sound of the speakers while you're recording and create a feedback loop. You should use headphones to listen as you record this project.

    Attach your microphone to the input of your audio interface. Check the Sound Device tab of the File > Preferences screen to make sure that your audio interface is selected. In the title bar of the first track, click the down arrow to the right of the Arm button to make sure the correct channel is selected for your audio interface. Select Monitor Incoming Audio if you need to hear what you are recording through the headphones. This may cause some unfortunate delay between what you say into the microphone and what you hear, so it is probably best to leave the Monitor Incoming Audio option unchecked.

3. Arm Track 1. Speak into the microphone to make sure you are getting a strong signal. Watch the volume readout in the first track to make sure the computer is able to hear you well. If you are getting a very weak signal, you may need to turn up the gain on the microphone input on your audio interface. If your signal is too strong, you may have to lower the level. Be aware that your proximity to the microphone is also a contributing factor to the strength of your sound. The microphone should be just a couple of inches from your mouth as you are speaking into it. Please note that is it never right to bang a microphone to see whether it's working. You can easily damage the microphone, headphones, speakers, and even your own hearing by doing that.

4. Press the Record button and start reading from the beginning of the following passage. If you make a mistake, press Stop and then listen back to what you've recorded. Find a place in the recording where you can cut in (probably between sentences or at places where you breathe) and delete anything after the cut-off moment (where the mistake is).

    You can delete easily by right-clicking in the track at the point where you wish to make the cut, selecting Split from the drop-down menu, and then deleting the region after the cut. You can also hold the mouse over the top-right corner of the region (the cursor will change to a double-headed arrow) and then click and drag the mouse back to where you wish to make the cut.

After you have made the cut, leave a couple of seconds of gap in the timeline, click in the track where you want to begin recording again, press Record, and then keep reading from the point at which you left off. Keep doing this until you have recorded the whole passage.

We interrupt this broadcast for some breaking news from the Tenth Annual Tongue-Tied Twister Club's Tongue Twister Tournament. The results are in. Competition was fierce this year, with a new champion crowned as the Supreme Winner of the Tongue-Tied Twister Club's Tongue Twister Cup. In third place this year was fan-favorite Fred Feather with his flawless rendition of "Red Leather Yellow Leather Red Leather Yellow Leather." Second place went to last year's winner, Peter Pepperpot, with his perfect performance of "Peter Piper Picked a Peck of Pickled Peppers." Peter Pepperpot performed well again this year but was pipped at the post by newcomer Josie Moseby, with her outrageously rapid recital of "Moses supposes his toeses are roses, but Moses supposes erroneously, for Moses he knowes his toeses aren't roses, as Moses supposes his toeses to be!" Phew! Now back to the studio.

---

5. Disarm the track. Press Rewind to Beginning and listen to what you have recorded. Click on the FX button beside the Arm button and add some effects to the channel. You might want to add in a compressor to smooth out the sound or perhaps a reverb. You might also like to add in the Acoustica EQ, which will give you more control over the EQ settings of your voice than the simple EQ in Mixcraft's Mixer tab will.

6. Trim the beginning and end of each clip in your recording so there's about a half-second before and after your recorded voice. Hold your mouse over the beginning of each clip, near the top, until it looks like a double-headed arrow. Click and hold, and then you can drag the start of the clip left or right. Try to line up the beginning of each clip with the moment your voice starts to read. Trim the end of each clip the same way.

7. Move the first clip close to the beginning of the track by dragging the region name. Leave a couple of seconds at the beginning. Drag the second clip to the end of the first clip so that the beginning half-second of the second clip overlaps the last half-second of the first clip.

    You may have to zoom in on the Sequencer window before doing this. You can zoom in and out easily by using the number pad +/− keys or by scrolling the mouse wheel up or down.

    When you overlap the clips, you will see that Mixcraft draws a big X over the overlapping regions. This is a crossfade, and it ensures that there won't be a popping sound between the clips as they play back. Listen to your recording from the beginning and adjust the overlap until it's in exactly the right place. Attach the rest of the clips to their predecessors by overlapping and cross-fading.

When you are happy with all of the crossfades, select all the clips in the track by selecting the first region and then clicking Edit > Select All (or use the shortcut key combination Ctrl+A). Now select Edit > Merge to New Clip (or use the shortcut key combination Ctrl+W).

8.   Now you are going to record some music for the beginning and end of your broadcast using your MIDI instrument (or Musical Typing). Find a good sound for Track 2 by clicking the Piano icon in the track. Arm the track and record a few seconds of music to introduce your broadcast. Remember, you can record different notes over a number of takes and merge the takes to a new clip by selecting Edit > Merge to New Clip (or using the shortcut key combination Ctrl+W). You can improvise some music or play some music you have already learned to play on the keyboard. (Many news broadcasts use snippets of pre-recorded music, so it's okay in this case to play something that somebody else composed.)

9.   Disarm the track when you are happy with your recording and then add some FX to it. Move the region in Track 1 so that the voice starts just as the music in Track 2 ends.

10.   Select the newly recorded passage by clicking on its name and then copy it to the end of the track. Select Edit > Copy or press Ctrl+C, scroll to the end of the track, click somewhere in Track 2 near the point at which the voice recording finishes, and select Edit > Paste or press Ctrl+V. Listen to the end of the recording and move the music clip to a good place so it starts just as the news bulletin ends.

11.   If you wish, you can add a fade-in and/or a fade-out to the MIDI recording, just as you did with the acoustic recording in "Alice's Adventures in Mixcraft." Click the Toggle Automation button to the left of the FX button in Track 2. Find a point where you would like the music in Track 2 to begin to fade and click on the horizontal line you see going through Track 2. Click again at the point where you would like the fade to end, hold the mouse button, and drag the point down. You will see you have created points on the line, and you now have a descending line between two of those points. This will fade out the music, just as you would do if you brought down the fader in the Mixer tab. Scroll to the end of the track and create a fade-in for the music and a fade-out for the news snippet.

12.   Listen to your work and check the levels of the voice and the music. The voice should always be audible, even when the music is playing. You can edit the level

of each, either in the automation lane or by using the Mixer tab. You can also pan your voice and MIDI recording slightly left and right—separating them slightly on either side of center is a good idea. Make sure nothing peaks into the red. When you are satisfied that your recording is the best that it can be, mix it down to an MP3 using File > Mix Down To > MP3. Make sure to play your recording of "The Tongue Twister Tournament" for friends or family members to see whether they like it.

Extensions

Write your own script for another segment of the news broadcast, record it, and add music to it. You can put together a number of broadcast segments in Mixcraft to create a longer news show. Drag the mixed-down MP3s directly into the Mixcraft window, lay them end to end in the same track, and crossfade them. Look ahead to Chapter 17 for ideas on how to publish your news broadcast online.

9 Recording Your Own Audio in GarageBand

This chapter contains two lessons to help you learn to record your own audio in GarageBand. Please see the companion DVD for a written tutorial on recording audio in GarageBand. The companion DVD also includes a video tutorial to help you with this chapter.

Lesson 1: Beat Box Composition *by Michael Fein*

National Standards

1. Singing, alone and with others, a varied repertoire of music

2. Performing on instruments, alone and with others, a varied repertoire of music

3. Improvising melodies, variations, and accompaniments

4. Composing and arranging music within specified guidelines

7. Evaluating music and music performances

Objectives

- Students will record themselves chanting various "beat box"–style sounds using a microphone.

- Students will arrange the beat-box sounds to create a rhythmic pattern.

- Students will add loops to the beat-box rhythmic pattern.

Class Time Required

You should be able to complete this lesson well in two one-hour sessions.

Materials

- "Production Central: The Other Side of the Glass" from *Electronic Musician* magazine. Available online at www.emusician.com/tutorials/production_central_other_side_glass.

■ Microphone and audio interface. Note that you may use the Mac's built-in microphone; however, you will achieve improved sound quality by using an audio interface and a professional microphone. See Chapter 3 for more information on using a microphone to record into GarageBand.

Preparations

1. Read the article from *Electronic Musician* magazine titled "Production Central: The Other Side of the Glass." Discuss the concepts presented about recording vocals.

2. Watch videos of people beat boxing. YouTube is a great resource for these types of videos. Try doing a search within YouTube for "beat box."

Procedure

1. Create a new GarageBand project using the Voice template in the QuickStart window (see Figure 9.1). Name the file Beat Box Composition and save it to your computer hard drive.

Figure 9.1 Use the Voice template in the QuickStart window.

2. Turn off Snap to Grid. (Choose Control > Snap to Grid or use the shortcut Command+G.)

3. Delete the two tracks created by GarageBand called Male Basic and Female Basic (press Command+Delete). These tracks are preloaded with some effects plug-ins, and I prefer to create Basic tracks without any preloaded effects to start recording.

4. Create a new Basic track (press Shift+Command+N).

5. Test your connection from your microphone to your computer by speaking into the microphone. You should see levels in the track bouncing up and down as you talk into the microphone.

Tip: If your track is not receiving any signal, try the following troubleshooting steps:

- Be sure the Record button on the track is lit red. **GarageBand '11 users note:** The Track Record button is hidden unless you select Track > Enable Multitrack Recording. In GarageBand '11, simply select a track to record into it.

- Turn up the Input Gain knob on your audio interface.

- If you are using the built-in microphone, turn up the Recording Level slider located in the Track Info pane (see Figure 9.2).

Figure 9.2   The Recording Level slider located in the Track Info pane.

- If you are using a condenser microphone, turn on the phantom power on your audio interface. The phantom power button is often named 48V on audio interfaces.

Tip: When recording, you want to achieve "good" levels. Be sure that your loudest levels do *not* go into the red area, as shown in Figure 9.3; this is known as *clipping*, and it will cause a distorted sound on your recording. It is also a good idea to avoid levels that are extremely soft, as shown in Figure 9.4; these will be difficult to edit and can introduce excessive noise into the recording. As in the story of Goldilocks and the three bears, you want it not too hot, but not too cold, as shown in Figure 9.5. I typically avoid using the Automatic Level Control built into GarageBand. I find that it is a better practice to set the levels properly from the start instead of trusting GarageBand to set the levels for you.

Figure 9.3   Clipping, too loud.

Figure 9.4   Too soft.

Figure 9.5   Good levels!

Tip: With vocal recordings, it is always best to use a pop filter to prevent level spikes caused by hard consonants, known as *plosives*.

---

6. Record a variety of beat box–style syllables into the first track. Review YouTube videos for some inspiration. You only need to record each syllable once; however, you can record a similar syllable with a different vocal inflection. It would be best to leave a small bit of silence between syllables to make the editing easier. See Figure 9.6.

Figure 9.6   Record a variety of beat box–style syllables into the first track.

Now you are going to chop up the syllables into individual regions so you can move and copy them into other tracks to create a beat-box rhythm.

7. Open the Track Editor.

8. Use the Marquee tool to select your first vocal syllable by clicking and dragging, as shown in Figure 9.7.

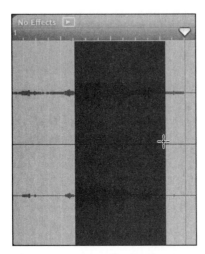

Figure 9.7   Use the Marquee tool to select your first vocal syllable.

9. Audition the selection by pressing Play. Be sure that you did not cut off part of the syllable. Reselect the material if you didn't select the entire syllable.

10. Click the selection, and GarageBand will turn it into a new region. Name the region so you will be able to identify it later in this project. See Figure 9.8.

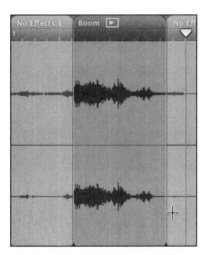

Figure 9.8   Click the selection and name the new region.

11. Repeat the previous step for all of your vocal syllables.

12. Delete any extraneous audio regions from the Arrange window. You may need to zoom in using the Zoom slider in the lower-left corner of the Arrange window. See Figure 9.9.

Figure 9.9   Delete extraneous audio regions.

13. Turn on Snap to Grid. (Select Control > Snap to Grid or use the shortcut Command+G.)

14. Turn on the Cycle tool and stretch the cycle so the yellow line goes from Bar 1 to Bar 9.

15. Duplicate the first Audio track by pressing Command+D. I suggest duplicating so that you have one track per syllable, so each syllable can reside on a single track.

16. Drag each syllable onto one of your new duplicate tracks.

17. Press Play and begin copying and/or moving regions to different locations in Bars 1 to 9 to create your rhythmic pattern. See Figure 9.10.

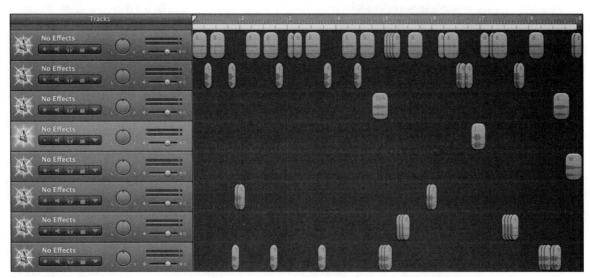

Figure 9.10 Copy and move regions to create an interesting rhythmic pattern.

Tip: When using Snap to Grid, the default grid value depends on your zoom level. To set a new grid value, click on the tiny ruler located in the upper-right corner of the Arrange window (see Figure 9.11). I suggest setting the grid value to 1/16.

Figure 9.11 The tiny ruler icon.

---

18. Open the Loop Browser and begin adding additional pitched loops to your composition. I suggest adding three or four pitched loops from categories such as bass, guitar, keyboard, synths, or strings.

19. Adjust the volume of each track to create a balanced blend of the various tracks.

20. Adjust the panning of each track to create an interesting stereo image. You can certainly create a lot of interest in the beat-box rhythm by panning different elements of the rhythm to different ears. See Figure 9.12.

21. Export the finished project by selecting Share > Send Song to iTunes or Share > Export Song to Disk.

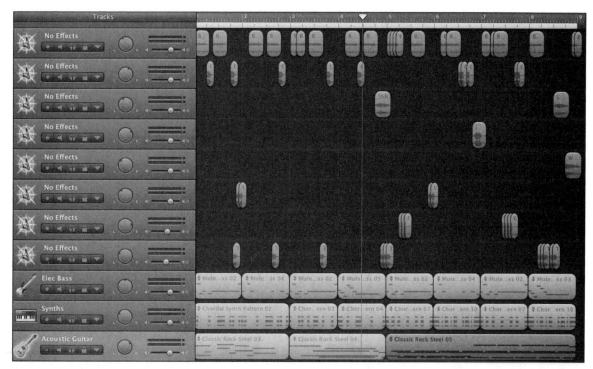

Figure 9.12 Add pitched loops to the composition and mix the file by adjusting the volume/panning of each track.

Extensions

Import percussion loops to enhance your beat-box rhythm. Try to perform improvised drum/percussion tracks. Compose a rap to accompany your beat-box composition and record it into a new track.

Tip: When you record with a microphone into a file that already has audio in it, be sure to use headphones so the microphone doesn't pick up sound from the computer's speaker output.

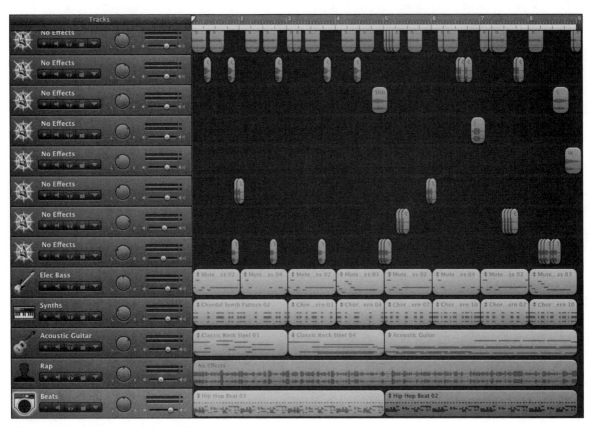

Figure 9.13 The completed file with the suggested extensions.

Lesson 2: Scene from Shakespeare *by Michael Fein*

National Standards

4. Composing and arranging music within specified guidelines

6. Listening to, analyzing, and describing music

8. Understanding relationships between music, the other arts, and disciplines outside the arts

9. Understanding music in relation to history and culture

Objectives

■ Recite a scene from a play by William Shakespeare.

■ Use effect plug-ins to alter the sound of the human voice.

■ Import Renaissance music to accompany the dialogue of the play.

Class Time Required

You should be able to complete this lesson well in two one-hour sessions.

Materials

■ The Complete Works of William Shakespeare website (shakespeare.mit.edu)

■ Wikipedia's William Shakespeare entry (en.wikipedia.org/wiki/William_Shakespeare)

■ Wikipedia's Renaissance Music entry (en.wikipedia.org/wiki/Renaissance_music)

Preparations

1. Students will read the Wikipedia entry on William Shakespeare to gain background knowledge on the famous playwright.

2. Students will read the Wikipedia entry on Renaissance music to gain background knowledge on the music popular during Shakespeare's life.

3. Students will visit The Complete Works of William Shakespeare website and select a play and then a scene to perform for this project. Print the text from the website to use as the script.

Procedure

1. Launch GarageBand and create a new project. Select Voice from the templates, name the file Scene from Shakespeare, and save the file to your desktop.

2. Delete the premade tracks (Male Basic and Female Basic).

3. Turn off the Snap to Grid feature (press Command+G).

4. Set the timeline to display minutes/seconds by clicking on the blue music note in the toolbar and selecting Time.

5. Create a new Basic track.

6. Check your levels to be sure that your input levels are not too loud or too soft. See the previous lesson in this chapter or Chapter 3 for more information on setting levels and connecting a microphone.

7. Recite the entire scene using only a single performer on a single track. See Figure 9.14.

Figure 9.14 Recite the entire scene using a single performer on a single track.

8. After recording, split the recorded region at the start of each new character's dialogue, as shown in Figure 9.15.

Figure 9.15 Split the recording at the start of each new character's dialogue.

9. Create additional new tracks. You will need one track per character in the scene.

10. Drag regions for each character into the new tracks. For example, if you selected a scene from *Romeo and Juliet*, all of Romeo's dialogue should reside on a new track, all of Juliet's dialogue should reside on a different new track, and so forth for the other characters.

Tip: Choose Control > Show Alignment Guides (or use the shortcut Shift+ Command+G). This will allow you to move regions vertically while maintaining their horizontal position.

Tip: Name the tracks by slowly clicking twice on the track name. (Each track is currently named "No Effects.") See Figure 9.16.

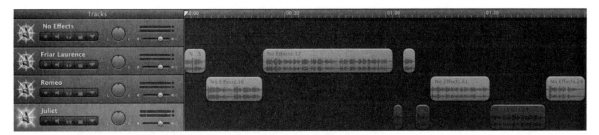

Figure 9.16 Drag regions for each character onto new tracks.

11. Click on the track for your first character.

12. Enable a cycle around the first region of dialogue by clicking the Cycle button in the toolbar and stretching the yellow bar in the timeline to fit the region.

13. Open the Track Info pane.

14. Select the Vocals category in the Track Info pane.

Tip: For Audio tracks (tracks with sound waves), the categories and settings in the Track Info pane refer to effect presets. For MIDI tracks (tracks with dots and dashes), the categories and settings refer to software instrument sounds *and* effect presents.

---

15. Press Play and begin trying out various effect presets. Your goal is to significantly change the sound of the voice while keeping it somewhat intelligible.

16. Repeat the previous step for all of your character tracks.

Tip: You can also design your own effect presets.

1. From the Vocals category, select No Effects, as shown in Figure 9.17.

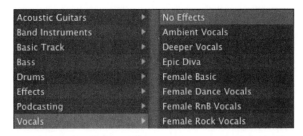

Figure 9.17 From the Vocals category, select No Effects.

2. Click the Edit tab in the Track Info pane.

3. Click an empty gray box in this window and select an effect.

4. Click on the effect plug-in icon to open the detailed effect plug-in window.

5. Adjust the settings manually or click Default and select a preset for that particular effect plug-in.

The most effective effect plug-in for this project is typically Vocal Transformer (see Figure 9.18).

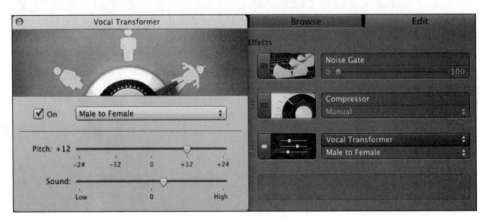

Figure 9.18   The Vocal Transformer effect plug-in.

17.   Play the file and adjust the volume for the various tracks. When you add effects to a track, you can often make the track dramatically softer or louder, so it is important to use the volume slider for each track to compensate.

18.   Adjust the panning of each track to provide an interesting stereo image. It would be unnatural to have all of the characters speaking at center stage, so be sure to pan some characters to varying degrees right and left, just as in a real theater production.

You are now going to add musical accompaniment to the scene. Based on your reading about Renaissance music, select something from this time period. Also, try to select music with an appropriate mood. If you selected a tragic scene, select music with a somber mood; if you selected a funny scene, select music with a lighter feel.

19.   Import Renaissance music into your GarageBand project.

Note: If you are importing music from a CD, insert the CD and use iTunes to import the files into your iTunes library. Any songs in iTunes are available in GarageBand by opening the Media Browser (see Figure 9.19). To import from the Media Browser, simply drag and drop into your Arrange window.

Figure 9.19   The Media Browser icon.

Note: If you are importing music from an MP3 file or a MIDI file, drag and drop the file from an open Finder window directly into your GarageBand project.

Tip: There are hundreds of excellent MIDI files of classical music available on the Internet. Try doing a Google search for "Renaissance MIDI" or "[*Name of Renaissance Composer*] MIDI." On most websites you can click a MIDI file to play it or right-click a MIDI file to download it to your hard drive.

Tip: When importing a MIDI file, GarageBand will do its best to select appropriate software instruments for each track. Feel free to select different software instruments for individual tracks by selecting the track and then selecting a new instrument in the Track Info pane.

20. Select Track > Show Master Track. A Master Track controls the overall sound output of the project. It is most often used to monitor volume levels and to create a fade-in or fade-out for the entire project.

21. Create a fade-in and fade-out for the entire project by clicking areas on the Master Volume line (see Figure 9.20).

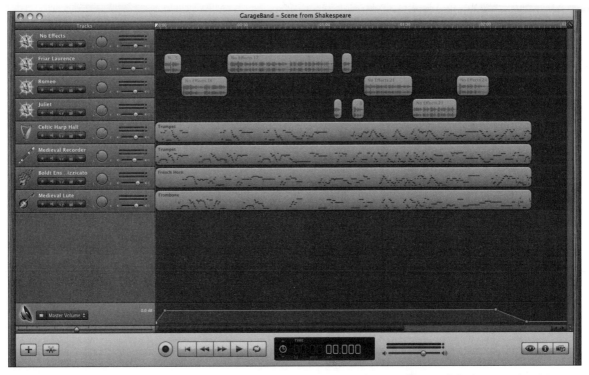

Figure 9.20 The completed project, including an imported MIDI file and fades on the Master Track.

22.   Export the finished project by selecting Share > Send Song to iTunes or Share > Export Song to Disk.

Extensions

Record an introduction to the scene in a new Basic track. This introduction should set up the project by explaining what has happened in the play prior to the scene.

Use volume automation to enhance the project. For example, if a character is supposed to be talking in the distance or offstage, automate the volume softer during those lines.

Tip: To view the volume automation for a particular track, click the down arrow under the track name. (**GarageBand '11 users note:** The down arrow is located to the right of the track name.) Similar to the Master Volume automation, click nodes on the Track Volume line to adjust the volume for the track. A value of 0.0 dB indicates standard volume, so going above this level will increase the volume, and going below this level will decrease the volume. In GarageBand, −144.0 dB indicates that the track is silent.

Record an additional scene in the same project, using the same character effect plug-in settings.

Perform the work for the class. Have students dress up and act out the scene as the GarageBand project plays.

10 Creating Podcasts in Mixcraft

This chapter contains two lessons to help you create podcasts in Mixcraft. Please see the companion DVD for a written tutorial on recording audio in Mixcraft, as well as a video tutorial.

Lesson 1: What's Your Opinion? *by Richard McCready*

National Standards

4. Composing and arranging music within specified guidelines

8. Understanding relationships between music, the other arts, and disciplines outside the arts

Objectives

- Prepare a podcast for your school news program in which you will interview other students about an important issue in your school.

- Record the students using Mixcraft, prepare a script to present their interview answers, find a jingle to introduce and finish the script, and then assemble all the parts together to make your podcast.

- Use the Trim Silence feature to remove unwanted silence and low-level noise from audio recordings.

Class Time Required

You should be able to complete this lesson well in three one-hour sessions, as well as one 90-minute session to record.

Materials

- Computer with Mixcraft installed

- Internet connection

- Headphones

- Microphone

- Audio interface

- Notepaper and pencils

- Six volunteers to write and record their answers to an interview question

Procedure

1. Think of an issue that might encourage other students to voice their opinions in a podcast. Maybe you could ask students about choices in the lunch menu, options for recess and after-school clubs, ideas for running student government, and so on. Choose a topic that you think other students would be interested in talking about and that encourages them to give an in-depth answer to a question about the topic. Design a short question that will allow students to air their opinion about the topic. Make sure your question encourages students to talk and is not answerable with a simple "yes" or "no" response. For example, you might ask, "What do you think the benefits might be of having healthier options to choose from in the daily lunch menu?" rather than "Do you like eating ice cream for lunch?"

2. Write down your question on notepaper, with space underneath for students to write down their answers. Copy the page enough times that you can give it out to six other students.

3. Choose six volunteers that you know will be able to answer the questions well. Tell them you're creating a podcast for the school news program, and you would like to record their answer to a short question for the broadcast. Give them each one of the question sheets and allow them some time to write down their responses. Collect the responses when they're ready.

4. Read through the responses for each question. If any of the volunteers has written something that you cannot include in the podcast, ask the student to rewrite his or her answer. Tell the volunteer you would very much like to feature his or her answer (that's why you asked in the first place) and give the student more time to come up with a new answer to the question. Do not reject any person you chose—give the volunteer another chance. You will only cause resentment if the student does not get represented in the podcast.

5. Create a schedule of when the volunteers can come to the Music Tech classroom/lab to record their interview answers. You will probably need about 15 minutes for each recording. If you can record everybody in one 90-minute session, that would be best, but if you have to schedule multiple sessions, that's okay, too. You'll just have to set up your microphone and audio interface for each session (and also tidy up afterward!).

6. On the day you record, set up your recording session 10 or 15 minutes before the first recording session is scheduled to start. Launch Mixcraft and select the top option (Record Yourself or Your Band) from the New Project screen.

Mixcraft will give you eight Audio tracks—exactly the number you will need for this project.

Connect a microphone to the audio interface. Change the names of Tracks 1 through 6 to the names of each of the people you're interviewing, in the order in which you are recording them. You can do this by double-clicking on each track name in the left pane of each track. Change the name of Track 7 to your own name. Change the name of Track 8 to "jingle." Save your work so far.

Mute all the tracks by clicking the Mute button under the track names. Check to make sure you are getting a signal from your microphone by arming one of the tracks and testing the mic. Disarm the track again after the test.

7. When the first volunteer arrives, make sure the correct source is selected in the drop-down menu beside the Arm button and then arm the track. Have the volunteer speak into the microphone to check the level. If you have selected the Monitor Incoming Audio option, you can unmute Track 1 and monitor the recording in the headphones as the volunteer speaks.

Find the sheet of notepaper that has the answer the volunteer wrote and place it somewhere where he or she can read it. When everything is ready, press Record and record the student reading the answer to the question. (You do not need to record the question.) Press Stop after the answer. (If you need to re-record the answer, you can press Ctrl+Z and Rewind to Beginning and then redo the recording.)

Disarm the track. Select the clip by clicking on its name bar and then click Sound > Trim Silence or use the shortcut key combination Ctrl+I. Listen back to the recording to make sure everything is good. If Mixcraft has trimmed a little too much at each end of the recording, you can drag the sides of the region out slightly to fix it.

Mute the track. Save your work. You might even consider saving to a flash drive or a network drive as well, so you have a backup copy. (You do not want to have to ask your volunteers to come back again if you lose or damage the file on which you are working.) Thank your volunteer for giving up his or her time to record.

8. Repeat Step 7 for each volunteer, until you have six recordings in the six tracks. You will be recording each student on consecutive tracks, so make sure you arm and unmute the correct tracks. You will be glad you named the tracks earlier.

9. Write a script to introduce and link your interview answers. You do not need to present the answers in the order they were recorded. Make sure you introduce the question you asked. For example, you could write, "Do you think we should have healthier choices on the lunch menu? I asked six students from our school this exact question, and here are their responses." Make sure you also

write segments in which you introduce each student by name before each recorded answer. Include a section where you summarize the volunteers' opinions and thank your listeners for listening to your podcast.

10.   Check to make sure Tracks 1 through 6 are muted. Arm Track 7 and record each section of your script. Press Stop after every segment you record, so that each part of the script has its own region in Track 7. If you need to re-record any section as you go, press Ctrl+Z to undo what you recorded and then record it again. Select each region in Track 7 by clicking on its name bar and then click Sound > Trim Silence or use the shortcut key combination Ctrl+I. Mute Track 7. Remember to save your work.

11.   Use the loop Library to find a loop you could use as a jingle to introduce and finish your podcast. Find something that will grab the listener's attention—trumpets, horns, loud guitars, and so on would work much better than drum beats. Drag the loop into Track 8. If Mixcraft asks you whether you would like to change the project tempo to match the loop, select No.

12.   Unmute all tracks. Move the jingle to the beginning of Track 8 if it is not already there. Move the first region in Track 7 so that it starts just as the jingle ends, but keep it in Track 7. Work through the whole script, aligning each part of the podcast so that each region begins just as the previous one ends. Do not drag the clips out of their original tracks, or Mixcraft will try to cross-fade them where they overlap. Listen to the podcast as you assemble it to make sure there are no times when there are long periods of silence (dead air) and no periods where two voices are speaking at the same time (cross talk). Copy the jingle clip from the beginning of the podcast to the end.

13.   In the Mixer tab, pan each of the volunteers' voices to different positions either side of center (three on the left, three on the right). Leave your own voice (Track 7) in the center pan position. Try to represent how it would sound if you had everybody sitting at one side of a table, with yourself in the middle and the microphone in the center of the table.

        Check the levels of each voice through the whole podcast so that there is a smooth transition between each recording. Some voices may be louder (or quieter) than others because they were closer to (or farther away from) the microphone, and you will have to compensate for that with your volume faders.

14.   If your recording sounds very dry, add a reverb to the FX section of the Master Mix fader. Make sure it is subtle enough that nobody would notice that you inserted the reverb unit. A golden rule of recording is that if people can hear an effect that you have inserted, you have inserted too much of that effect. Mix down your podcast by selecting File > Mix Down To > MP3. Ask your school principal if he or she will listen to your podcast and consider letting you play it on the school news.

Extensions

Find out whether you can make your podcasts a regular feature on the school news broadcasts or whether you would be allowed to submit some podcasts to be included on the school website or the student government website. If you do this, you may start to create a following. Students might come to you with suggestions of questions for future podcasts or to volunteer to have their opinions heard in your podcasts. Keep your podcasts short. It is better to have regular podcasts of one to two minutes than to have sporadic podcasts lasting 10 minutes or more. You will become very skilled at making podcasts as you gain experience. Look ahead to Chapter 17 for ideas on how to publish your podcasts online.

Lesson 2: Let's Hear It for Local Music
by Richard McCready

National Standards

6. Listening to, analyzing, and describing music

7. Evaluating music and music performances

8. Understanding relationships between music, the other arts, and disciplines outside the arts

9. Understanding music in relation to history and culture

Objectives

- Record a podcast review of an album by a local band, musical group, or musician. (An album is a collection of songs put together by an artist as a related collection. By podcasting the album review, you will be able to help the local artist by drawing attention to his or her music.) Extract the files from the CD, edit the album tracks in Mixcraft to create short excerpts, and write and record a script to describe the album.

- Record your script and assemble the podcast with cross-fades.

- Learn how to print a track to a new Audio track to make effects settings permanent without needing to keep effects plug-ins active.

Copyright Note

Please note that to do this project, you will need to find an album that you can get permission to review. Some students in your school might be in a band, or they may compose music on their computers at home. They may be more than happy to give you a CD of their songs to review. They could also make copies of the songs on a flash drive for you. Or, you may have friends or relatives outside of school who are in a band or a musical group and who could help you out by giving you an album for this project.

If you want to review an album put out by a commercial company, you first have to obtain permission from the recording company to make the podcast, as you will need to use excerpts of the songs, and the songs are copyrighted. There is no way around this—it is the law. If you send a letter or an email to the company asking permission, they might grant it to you, especially if you tell them you're podcasting the review for a school project. It is not legal to use excerpts of music in a podcast unless you have permission from the copyright owner, even if the excerpts are short.

Class Time Required

You should be able to complete this lesson well in three one-hour sessions, but you will also need to spend some time outside of class collecting information, listening to the album, and writing your review of it.

Materials

- Computer with Mixcraft installed

- Internet connection

- Headphones

- Microphone

- Audio interface

- Notepaper and pen or pencil

- Copy of an album on CD or a copy of the music files on a flash drive

Procedure

1. Find an album to review. You probably will need to ask musical friends or relatives whether they will let you have a CD of their band or musical group to review. Do not choose a commercially released album unless you have already been given permission to review the album. See the section about copyright earlier in this chapter.

2. Listen to the album all the way through several times to familiarize yourself with the songs. Read through the lyrics. You may find them in the CD liner notes or on the band's website, or you can ask the musicians to let you see a copy of the lyrics. Choose carefully, and make sure the album you select for this project is appropriate for school. There should be no profanity, no racism or sexism, and no lyrics that denigrate people because of their religion, beliefs, politics, or sexuality. If you are unsure about whether an album is acceptable, it probably is not. If there is something in the lyrics that you think might offend, it more than likely will. You may want to double-check with an adult—perhaps a teacher or a parent.

3. If you have the album on CD, rip the files onto the computer using iTunes, Windows Media Player, or other CD-ripping software. Make sure you know where the files are stored on the computer once they are ripped. If you have the files on a flash drive, transfer them to the computer you are using for this project. No matter whether you rip the songs from the CD or transfer them from a flash drive, you will need to keep them in a folder you can easily access on the computer desktop. Create a folder on the desktop by right-clicking the desktop and selecting New > Folder, name the folder, and copy the audio files to the folder. Move the folder to a corner of the desktop where you can access it easily.

4. Write a review of your chosen album as a podcast script. You should probably use notepaper and a pen or pencil to write your script. If you try to use a

program on the computer to do this, you'll find yourself running out of screen real estate when you start working in Mixcraft. It is also a good idea not to have other programs open when you are working in Mixcraft, so it would be counter productive for you to have word processing or text programs open as you are assembling your podcast.

You might like to start writing your podcast by finding out some information about the band or the musician. Find some time to talk to the people who recorded the music. Collect some information that people would find interesting and begin your podcast script with a section where you talk briefly about the musicians. Write a couple of sentences where you focus on the album itself—maybe some information about when and how it was recorded or what the artists wanted to achieve in recording the album. Then focus on the individual tracks. Write a couple of short sentences for each track, describing it or giving your listeners something to observe in each song on the album. Write a conclusion encouraging your listeners to buy the album and listen to it or to go see this band or musician play live. You might include details of the band's next concert.

5. Listen to each track on the album again and find a section of each song that you can play in your podcast to illustrate the points you are making in the script. Make note of the times of each excerpt. Each excerpt you choose should be short. It is a good idea to use excerpts that are less than 20 seconds.

6. Launch Mixcraft and select the top option (Record Yourself or Your Band) from the New Project screen. Mixcraft will give you eight Audio tracks. You might need to add Audio tracks for this project, as you will need one track for each of the songs on the album, one track for voice recording, and one track for podcast assembly. So, if your album has eight tracks, you will need 10 Audio tracks in Mixcraft for this project. Use Track > Add Track > Audio Track or the shortcut key combination Ctrl+G to add the tracks you need.

7. Alter the size of the Mixcraft window so you can see the folder of audio files you placed on the desktop earlier. Open the desktop folder, select the first track, and drag it into the first track in Mixcraft. Trim the audio file to the excerpt you need by holding and dragging the sides of the audio region. Leave a couple of seconds on each side of the excerpt for fade-in and fade-out. You can use the Zoom function (+/− keys on the number pad or the mouse scroll wheel) to help you zoom in on the excerpt so you can edit more precisely.

When you move the sides of the region, you are not deleting anything—you are just letting Mixcraft know what part of the excerpt to play. You can keep moving the ends of the region left and right until you get the precise excerpt you want. After you have completed all the editing on the first track, mute it. Then drag the second album track into the second track in Mixcraft and edit it. Mute it when you have completed the editing. Keep repeating this process until you have added all the tracks from the album into their own tracks in Mixcraft and you have edited them. Maximize the Mixcraft window again.

8. Change the name of the next track in Mixcraft to "Voice Recording." Connect your microphone to the audio interface, check your input source, arm the track, and check your recording level. When everything is set up, record your script. Record it in sections, pressing Stop after every section and leaving a gap before recording the next one. You can undo recordings and rerecord by pressing Ctrl+Z to undo. When you have finished recording the whole script, select every region of your recorded script individually by clicking on its title bar and select Sound > Trim Silence. You need to do this for each audio region in your podcast.

9. Listen to the voice recording the whole way through to make sure everything is good. Rerecord if necessary. Click the FX button in the left pane of the track and add an EQ, a compressor, and a reverb to the track. Choose presets for the effects modules or tweak the preset settings to create a good, strong sound for your voice.

   You now need to print the voice recording to a new track—you cannot add these effects in the Master Fader or the Podcast Assembly track, or you will alter the sound of the musical excerpts. Select everything in the Voice Recording track by first selecting one region and then choosing Edit > Select All or using the shortcut key combination Ctrl+A. Select Track > Mix to New Audio Track. Mixcraft will now add a new track to the Sequencer window with your effects added into the sound. Mixcraft will also mute your original voice track for you.

   Listen to the new track. Even though there are no effects units on this new track (the FX button is not selected), you can hear the effects you added in the original track! You can delete the original voice track if you want, though it may be best to keep it in case you want to redo the effects later.

10. Change the name of the last track to "Podcast Assembly." Drag the first part of the recorded script into the track and align it with the beginning of the timeline. Assemble the podcast in the track in the order you want the excerpts to appear. When you drag a musical excerpt in, you can overlap it with the spoken section before it to create an automatic cross-fade—the music will fade in as the voice fades out. Then when you drag in the next spoken section, you can overlap again so the music fades out as the voice fades in.

   Sometimes the cross-fade might not be exactly what you're looking for, as the voice may get lost as the music fades in. An alternative way to create fades is to drag the mouse over the first few seconds of the excerpt, select Sound > Fade In, and choose a fade speed. You can create fade-outs with the Sound > Fade Out selection. Experiment with the fade speeds and with overlapping regions to get the effect you want.

11.   Make sure all tracks are muted except for the Podcast Assembly track. Listen to the whole podcast and check to make sure the Master Mix fader does not peak into the red. Mix down your podcast by selecting File > Mix Down To > MP3. Play your podcast for the band members or the musicians who gave you their music. Ask your music teacher whether he or she will let you play your podcast for the other students in your music class. If you asked a friend or a relative outside of school to help you find an album, make sure you let that person hear your podcast—he or she will doubtless be interested to hear your review.

Extensions

Create a jingle for the beginning and end of your podcast by using the loops in Mixcraft, or choose a different excerpt from the album you reviewed. Review some other albums by the same artist and make a series of podcasts. When other bands and musicians start to hear that you are making podcast reviews, they may start coming to you with their albums and ask you to create podcasts. All bands and musicians know that they need publicity for their music, so you are definitely helping them out by promoting their music and their concerts. Look ahead to Chapter 17 for ideas on how to publish your podcasts online.

11 Creating Podcasts in GarageBand

This chapter contains two lessons to help you create podcasts in GarageBand. Please see the companion DVD for a written tutorial on creating podcasts in GarageBand. The companion DVD also includes a video tutorial to help you with this chapter and Chapter 13.

Lesson 1: This Day in History *by Michael Fein*

National Standards

4. Composing and arranging music within specified guidelines

6. Listening to, analyzing, and describing music

8. Understanding relationships between music, the other arts, and disciplines outside the arts

9. Understanding music in relation to history and culture

Objectives

- Use the Internet to research events that occurred on a specific date.

- Write a short essay describing the most important events from the selected date.

- Record the script using a microphone and GarageBand software.

- Import music and images to accompany the podcast.

Class Time Required

You should be able to complete this lesson well in three one-hour sessions.

Materials

- Essay Framework.pdf file located on the companion DVD

Preparations

1. Research important events that occurred on a specific date. Some excellent websites include:

    - Wikipedia (en.wikipedia.org/wiki/Main_Page).

- Library of Congress's Today in History Archives (memory.loc.gov/ammem/today/archive.html).

- The People History (www.thepeoplehistory.com).

- Google (www.google.com). Try searching the specific day in quotes. For example, search "February 2."

2. Complete the Essay Framework.pdf file located on the companion DVD to help narrow the topics. Include additional events, births, deaths, or other relevant information as you see fit.

3. Write the podcast script based on the essay framework created in Step 2. Be sure to include opening and closing remarks.

- Opening remark example: "Hello and welcome to *This Day in History*. My name is _____ (first name only for students), and my podcast will focus on important events, births, and deaths that occurred on February 2nd throughout history."

- Closing remark example: "Thank you for taking the time to listen to my podcast."

Procedure

1. Launch GarageBand and create a new project using the Podcast template (see Figure 11.1). Name the file This Day in History and save it to the desktop.

Figure 11.1 Select the Podcast template from the QuickStart window.

2. Delete the Male Voice and Female Voice tracks (press Command+Delete).

3. Create a new Basic track (press Shift+Command+N).

4. Record your script into the new Basic track. For detailed instructions on recording audio into GarageBand see Chapters 3 and 9. Be sure to record with good levels—not too soft and certainly no clipping.

Tip: If you stumble over a word during your recording, don't scrap the recording and start over! After a stumble, allow GarageBand to continue recording, pause and compose yourself, and begin recording one sentence before the stumble. After you finish recording, you can split the region around the stumble, delete the bad region, and move the good region over so the speech flows smoothly.

This Day in History – Essay Framework

Important Event 1: _____

Brief Description: _____

_____

_____

Important Event 2: _____

Brief Description: _____

_____

_____

Important Event 3: _____

Brief Description: _____

_____

_____

****

Important Birth 1: _____

Brief Description: _____

_____

_____

Important Birth 2: _____

Brief Description: _____

_____

_____

Important Birth 3: _____

Brief Description: _____

_____

_____

****

Important Death 1: _____

Brief Description: _____

_____

_____

Important Death 2: _____

Brief Description: _____

_____

_____

Important Death 3: _____

Brief Description: _____

_____

_____

5. Open the Track Info pane and add one of the effect presets from the Vocals category. I suggest trying Male Basic or Female Basic. These effect presets use a combination of EQ, compression, and reverb to subtly improve the sound of dialogue. You can also develop your own effect preset; see the lesson titled "Scene from Shakespeare" in Chapter 9 for detailed instructions on using effect presets.

    You are now going to import music to accompany your podcast. I recommend using Jingles (royalty-free songs included with GarageBand) to avoid any copyright concerns. Before adding in music, try to divide the script into three to five sections. For example, you may have the following sections in your script: intro, events, births, deaths, closing. You will want to use a different jingle for each section.

6. Open the Loop Browser. Click on the Podcast icon (which is most likely already selected) and then click on Jingles, as shown in Figure 11.2.

Figure 11.2 Click the Podcast icon and select Jingles.

7. Select a jingle category and click on various jingles in the bottom portion of the Loop Browser to preview the jingle.

8. Drag a jingle into the Jingles track.

9. Repeat the previous step for the other sections of your script.

Tip: If one section of your voice recording lasts longer than the jingle, loop the jingle to repeat it.

---

10. Create a rough mix by listening to the file and adjusting the volume of the Jingles track. You want the music audible, but you certainly do not want the music to overpower the voice recording.

Tip: Ducking is a great feature in GarageBand that automatically turns down the volume of secondary tracks whenever audio is playing from primary tracks. Secondary tracks are indicated by downward-pointing blue arrows, and primary tracks are indicated by upward-pointing yellow arrows (see Figures 11.3 and Figures 11.4).

Figure 11.3 A downward-pointing arrow indicates a secondary track.

Figure 11.4 An upward-pointing arrow indicates a primary track.

11. Fade in and out of each jingle region using automation (see Figure 11.5).

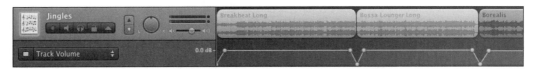

Figure 11.5 Fade in and out of each jingle region using automation.

12. An enhanced podcast includes images that accompany the audio. Search the Internet for relevant images. You will need at least one image per topic for your podcast. I suggest doing a Google search and then selecting Images in the upper-left corner of the browser to see only images related to your search. Click on an image and then be sure to select Full-Size Image.

13. Drag the image from the website to your desktop. You can also place the image on your desktop by right-clicking (or Control-clicking) the image and selecting Save Image As.

14. Drag the image from your desktop to the Podcast track of the GarageBand project. You can also drag images directly into GarageBand; however, I typically avoid doing this because if you accidentally delete the image in Garage-Band, you will have to find the image on the Internet again.

Tip: Here's my favorite way to copy a picture into GarageBand:

1. Open the GarageBand file.

2. Click on the Finder icon on your Dock. This will open a new Finder window.

3. Navigate to the desktop and locate the image file.

4. Drag the image file into the Podcast track in GarageBand.

I find this much easier than trying to move the GarageBand window around to locate the picture hiding under it on the desktop.

15.   Continue dragging image files for each topic into the GarageBand Podcast track.

16.   Use the Trim tool to stretch or shorten an image. I recommend having the images right next to each other. See Figure 11.6.

Figure 11.6   Place the images right next to each other.

Tip: If the image is not perfectly square, you may need to resize it to make it fit correctly in the Podcast track. Click the Podcast track and then open the Track Editor. Double-click the image in the Track Editor to open up the Artwork Editor. Zoom into the image by adjusting the zoom bar at the bottom of the window and reposition the image by dragging. When you are finished, click Set. See Figure 11.7.

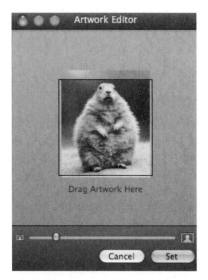

Figure 11.7   Resize or reposition the image in the Artwork Editor.

17.   Listen to the file and evaluate the finished product.

- Can you clearly hear the voice, or is the music too loud?
- Does the music fade in and out smoothly?

■ Look at the Preview icon in the Podcast track while you listen to the file. Do the images change appropriately? Is there always an image displayed, or do you have sections that display "No Artwork Available?"

18. Export your finished file by selecting Share > Send Podcast to iTunes, as shown in Figure 11.8. You can also select Export Podcast to Disk to save the file to your desktop instead of to the iTunes Library.

Figure 11.8 Export the file by selecting Share > Send Podcast to iTunes.

Extensions

Instead of using jingles for your background audio, try composing your own music.

■ Use loops only, or

■ Record your MIDI keyboard to compose original music, or

■ Use a microphone to record acoustic instruments, such as guitar, saxophone, vocals, and so on, or

■ Use a combination of acoustic instruments, MIDI keyboard tracks, and loops

Lesson 2: AM Radio Show *by Michael Fein*

National Standards

4. Composing and arranging music within specified guidelines

6. Listening to, analyzing, and describing music

8. Understanding relationships between music, the other arts, and disciplines outside the arts

9. Understanding music in relation to history and culture

Objectives

■ Compose a script for the AM Radio Show, including news headlines, weather, sports, and traffic.

■ Record the script using a microphone and GarageBand software.

■ Import music and images to accompany the podcast.

Class Time Required

You should be able to complete the lesson well in three one-hour sessions.

Materials

■ Script Framework.pdf located on the companion DVD

Preparations

1. Listen to an actual AM news radio show. For example, in Philadelphia, tune to 1060 AM. In New York, tune to 1010 AM. Most news radio shows play a loop of news every 10 minutes in the morning. This loop includes news headlines, weather, sports, and traffic.

2. Complete the Script Framework.pdf file to organize your ideas for the Radio Show script.

Note: Use the Internet to complete your framework with as much real information as possible. For example, visit www.weather.com for weather forecast information and www.reuters.com for national/global news headlines and stories.

---

3. Write the podcast script based on the framework created in Step 2 of the "Preparations" section.

Procedure

1. Launch GarageBand and create a new project using the Podcast template (see Figure 11.9). Name the file AM Radio Show and save it to the desktop.

Figure 11.9 Select the Podcast template from the QuickStart window.

AM Radio Show – Script Framework

1. Local News Headlines:

    a.

    b.

    c.

2. National/Global News Headlines:

    a.

    b.

    c.

3. Today's Weather Forecast:

4. 5-Day Weather Forecast:

5. Sports Results/News:

    a.

    b.

    c.

6. Traffic:

7. Other:

    a.

    b.

    c.

2. Delete the Male Voice and Female Voice tracks (press Command+Delete).

3. Create a new Basic track (press Shift+Command+N).

4. Record your script into the new Basic track. For detailed instructions on recording audio into GarageBand, refer to Chapters 3 and 9. Be sure to record with good levels!

Tip: If you are completing this project in a group, use a new Basic track for each person.

---

5. Open the Track Info pane and add one of the effect presets from the Vocals category. See the lesson titled "This Day in History" from earlier in this chapter or the lesson titled "Scene from Shakespeare" from Chapter 9 for detailed instructions on using effect presets and suggested settings.

6. Open the Arrange Track by clicking Track > Show Arrange Track (see Figure 11.10).

Figure 11.10 Select Track > Show Arrange Track.

7. Click twice slowly on "untitled" in the Arrange Track and name the section "Introduction."

8. Move your cursor to the left corner of this Arrange section and stretch the bar to the end of your introduction.

9. Add a new Arrange section by clicking the plus icon in the Arrange Track.

10. Repeat Steps 7 through 9 for all remaining sections (local news headlines, national/global news headlines, weather forecast, and so on). See Figure 11.11.

0:00	02:00	04:00	06:00	08:00	10:00
Arrangement:	Introduction	Local News	National/Global News	Today's Weather	5-day Forecast	Sports	Traffic

Figure 11.11 Name each section in the Arrange Track.

11. Open the Loop Browser. Click on the Podcast icon (which is most likely already selected) and then click on Jingles (see Figure 11.12).

12. Select a jingle category and click on various jingles in the bottom portion of the Loop Browser to preview them.

13. Drag a jingle into the Jingles track.

Figure 11.12 Click the Podcast icon and select Jingles.

14. Repeat the previous step for the other sections of your script so that each section has its own musical accompaniment.

15. Create a rough mix by listening to the file and adjusting the volume of the Jingles track. You want the music audible, but you certainly do not want it to overpower the voice recording. Remember that the Jingles track is set to get softer when audio is played from the new Basic tracks. This is called *ducking*; refer to the project titled "This Day in History" from earlier in this chapter.

16. Fade in and out of each jingle region using automation (see Figure 11.13).

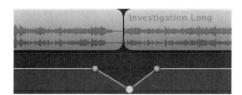

Figure 11.13 Fade in and out of each jingle region using automation.

17. Search the Internet for relevant images. Refer to the lesson titled "This Day in History" from earlier in this chapter for tips on downloading images.

18. Drag the images from your desktop to the Podcast track of the GarageBand project. You should have at least one image per section. Use your Arrange Track as a guide and be sure to use the Trim tool to stretch or shorten the images.

19. Listen to the file and evaluate the finished product.

   ▪ Can you clearly hear the voice, or is the music too loud?

   ▪ Does the music fade in and out smoothly?

   ▪ Look at the Preview icon in the Podcast track while you listen to the file. Do the images change appropriately? Is there always an image displayed, or do you have sections that display "No Artwork Available?"

20. Export your finished file by selecting Share > Send Podcast to iTunes. You can also select Export Podcast to Disk to save the file to your desktop instead of the iTunes Library.

Extensions

Instead of using jingles for background music, compose your own music using loops, the MIDI keyboard, and/or acoustic instruments.

Develop a logo for your radio show. The logo should include the station frequency, the show name, and an image. I suggest using Microsoft PowerPoint or Apple Keynote to develop the logo.

1. Create a new presentation in PowerPoint or Keynote.

2. In PowerPoint, select Title Slide from the New Slide window. In Keynote, select a theme.

3. Enter the station frequency in one text box and the show name in the other text box.

4. Drag an image from your web browser into the title slide and size it appropriately.

5. Experiment with fonts, layout, background color, and so on to finalize your logo (see Figure 11.14).

Figure 11.14 An example logo design.

6. In PowerPoint, select File > Save As. In Keynote, select File > Export.

7. In the Save or Export dialog box, click the pop-up window next to Format and select JPEG.

8. Name the file AM Radio Show LOGO and save it or export it to your desktop.

9. Drag the JPEG image into the Episode Artwork section located in the Track Editor for the Podcast track in GarageBand, as shown in Figure 11.15. This image will now display any time there is no image in the Podcast track. You may want to trim the first and last images of the file so your logo will display at the start and end of your file.

Figure 11.15 Drag the JPEG image into the Episode Artwork section located in the Track Editor for the Podcast track in GarageBand.

12 Working with Video in Mixcraft

This chapter contains two lessons to help you learn how to work with video in Mixcraft. Please see the companion DVD for a written tutorial on working with video in GarageBand, as well as a video tutorial.

Lesson 1: The Marathon of Fright *by Richard McCready*

National Standards

2. Performing on instruments, alone and with others, a varied repertoire of music

3. Improvising melodies, variations, and accompaniments

4. Composing and arranging music within specified guidelines

8. Understanding relationships between music, the other arts, and disciplines outside the arts

Objectives

- Compose or improvise a soundtrack for a trailer for a vintage horror movie entitled *The Marathon of Fright*.

- Import video files into Mixcraft.

- Use Mixcraft's synthesizers to create some spooky sounds.

- Write and record narration.

- Mix down your project to a movie file.

Class Time Required

You should be able to complete this lesson well in three one-hour sessions.

Materials

- Computer with Mixcraft installed

- Internet connection

- Headphones

- MIDI keyboard

- Microphone

- Audio interface

- Notepaper and pencils

- Video for Marathon of Fright.avi file from the companion DVD

Procedure

1. Launch Mixcraft and select the top option (Record Yourself or Your Band) from the New Project screen. You will probably only need one Audio track, so delete the others. Add two Virtual Instrument tracks by selecting Track > Add Track > Virtual Instrument Track (or use the shortcut key combination Ctrl+E). Save your file and remember to keep saving every few minutes as you work.

2. Select Video > Add a Video File and locate the video entitled Video for Marathon of Fright. It will take a few moments for Mixcraft to import the video and create thumbnails in the Video track; please be patient.

   After the movie has completely loaded, click Show Video Window in the track's name bar. Press Play and watch the video. You can hide the video window whenever you need to free up screen real estate during this project. You will notice that the Show Video Window button reads Hide Video Window when the video window is open. You can also resize the video window at any time by dragging its corners with the mouse.

3. Think of the type of music that might go well with the video. Horror movie soundtracks are full of spooky sounds and low, slow notes that gradually get faster as tension builds. (Think of the theme from *Jaws*, for example.) Click the Piano icon in the name bar of one of the Instrument tracks, select the second option in the left pane, <VSTi Instruments>, and select Alien 303 Bass Synthesizer. The window will open to show the Alien 303 listed in the virtual instrument details section. Play some notes on your MIDI keyboard, and you should be able to hear the Alien 303 through your headphones.

   Try some of the presets or press Edit beside the listed presets, and you will see the controls for the Alien 303 itself. You may need to move or resize the video window to see the Alien 303. Choose a sound you can work with and tweak some of the knobs to shape your own sound.

4. Press Play and compose/improvise some low, slow sounds on your MIDI keyboard as you watch the video. Speed up your music as the movie progresses. When you are ready to record, arm the track, press Rewind to Beginning and then Record, and perform your composition/improvisation along with the

video. Listen back to your track. If you are satisfied with your recording, disarm the track. If you need to rerecord, press Ctrl+Z and Rewind to Beginning and Record again.

5.   Click the Piano icon in the second Instrument track and select Impulse from the <VSTi Instruments> category. Try some presets by playing your MIDI keyboard or use the Edit button to bring up the Impulse interface. Try playing several notes together to see what happens in Impulse. Press Play and compose/improvise some note clusters and chords on your MIDI keyboard as you watch the video. You should be able to hear the previously recorded sounds of the Alien 303 in your headphones as you play your MIDI keyboard through Impulse.

When you are ready to record, arm the track, press Rewind to Beginning and then Record, and perform your composition/improvisation along with the video. Listen back to your track. If you are satisfied with your recording, disarm the track. If you need to rerecord, press Ctrl+Z and Rewind to Beginning and Record again.

6.   If you wish to add more Instrument tracks to your soundtrack, you can. You could try the MinimogueVA or the VB3 Organ from the <VSTi Instruments> category. If you play an acoustic instrument or an electric guitar, you could also record yourself by creating an Audio track and playing through a microphone or with a cable connected directly to your audio interface from your guitar. Make sure that the correct channel is selected for your input and that your recording levels are good. Try to make your instrument sound really weird as you improvise or compose some music to add to your soundtrack.

7.   Listen to your work so far. Add some reverb and other effects in the FX chain for each of your instruments. Automate some volume changes by using the automation lanes and experiment with automating some panning settings. You can add a lot of atmosphere to your soundtrack by making your sounds move between the left and right channels.

8.   Using notepaper and a pen or pencil, write a short narration for the movie trailer for *The Marathon of Fright*. You can use some of the passages that you read on the screen during the trailer and add some of your own. Be concise: This is a short trailer, and it is better to leave gaps in the narration than to have too much material you need to squeeze in.

9.   Record your narration on an Audio track using your microphone and audio interface. It is wiser (though slower) to record the script in short sections than to do so in one long take. Remember to use Ctrl+I to trim the silence of each clip. After the script is recorded, you can move the sections into the correct place on

the timeline. The thumbnails on the Video track will help you place your narration clips in the correct place.

10.   Add a compressor to your recorded Audio track to smooth out your voice. Add some reverb and EQ to make your voice sound big and spooky.

11.   Use the Mixer tab to mix your movie soundtrack together. While you mix, you should probably hide the video window so you can concentrate on listening to how the sounds balance together. Make sure the voice is heard at all times and be prepared to cut the sounds of the instruments so that the listener can hear the narration clearly. Have a friend listen to make sure the voice is audible throughout the soundtrack.

12.   Mix down your movie by selecting File > Mix Down To > AVI. You will now be able to watch the completed video on your computer using Windows Media Player or QuickTime. It would be fun to project the movie from the computer to a big screen using an LCD projector and play the soundtrack through the classroom speakers. Remember to turn out the lights for the full horror movie experience!

Extensions

You can view and download many old movies and trailers at www.archive.org. Search through the Moving Images category at the website and see whether you can find some short movies to which you could add soundtracks. Everything that is downloadable at www.archive.org is in the public domain, so you do not need to apply for copyright permission to publish your movies online.

Lesson 2: LEGO Spider-Man *by Richard McCready*

National Standards

2. Performing on instruments, alone and with others, a varied repertoire of music

3. Improvising melodies, variations, and accompaniments

4. Composing and arranging music within specified guidelines

6. Listening to, analyzing, and describing music

8. Understanding relationships between music, the other arts, and disciplines outside the arts

Objectives

■ Compose a movie soundtrack for a Spider-Man video, created completely with LEGO blocks.

■ Learn to edit and cross-fade video in Mixcraft.

■ Learn how to use the sound effects library in Mixcraft and how to alter the effects to create even more sounds.

■ Learn to freeze tracks to help preserve computer processing power.

Class Time Required

This is a big project. You should be able to complete this lesson well in four or five one-hour sessions, but you may need more time to get really creative.

Materials

■ Computer with Mixcraft installed.

■ Internet connection.

■ Headphones.

■ You can use a MIDI keyboard and/or acoustic instruments if you wish, though you can complete this project easily without them.

■ Microphone.

■ Audio interface.

■ Notepaper and pen or pencil.

■ Video for Spiderman.avi file from the companion DVD.

Procedure

1. Launch Mixcraft and select the top option (Record Yourself or Your Band) from the New Project screen. You will need many Audio tracks for this project, so do not delete the tracks Mixcraft gives you. Select Video > Add a Video File and locate the video entitled Video for Spiderman. After the movie has completely loaded, click Show Video Window in the track's name bar. Press Play and watch the video. Save your file and remember to keep saving every few minutes as you work.

2. Try to work out what the story of the video is. You will be able to add sound effects, narration/voice, and music to it, but you will need to plan a story. If there is a section of the movie you cannot use in your story, you can edit it out very easily in Mixcraft. Decide on a place where you want to make a cut. You will need to split the track twice, at each end of your cut. It is best to leave a couple of seconds on either side of the region you want to cut so you have room to cross-fade the video.

   Right-click on the Video track's name bar at each point where you want to make a cut and select Split from the drop-down menu (or left-click on the cut point and use the shortcut key combination Ctrl+T). Select the clip you wish to remove and delete it. Then drag the later region onto the first region until they overlap. You will see that Mixcraft automatically creates a cross-fade for you. Watch the segment of the video where you made the cut and observe how smoothly Mixcraft makes this happen.

3. Using notepaper and a pen or pencil, write down the plan for your story and note the times in the script where you might like to include some narration/voices and sound effects. There are many opportunities in this video for adding sounds.

   Open the Library tab at the bottom of the Mixcraft window and change the category to Sound Effect. You will see that there are more than 1,300 sound effects you can add to your movie. It is probably easiest to browse through them if you undock the Library first—you will see the Undock button at the top right of the Library Browser. Now you will be able to move and resize the Library window.

   Scroll down the window and listen to some effects. As you hear effects you can use for your movie, drag them from the Library Browser into the Sequencer window. Don't worry about lining them up with the movie yet—you can do that after you have found several good sound effects. Drag each effect into a new track. If you need to add more Audio tracks, use Track > Add Track > Audio Track or the shortcut key combination Ctrl+G.

4. Close the Library Browser. Using the times you noted on your notepaper, line up the sound effects to the correct point in the movie. Using the FX button on the track name, add some audio effects to each track. You'll find that you can create some very cool results if you experiment. For example, if you have the Laser effect on a track, add in the Classic Flanger using the Bucket on Head preset and the Classic Reverb using the Grand Hall preset. Listen to the result—it's even more laser-like than the original effect.

Take time to experiment with every sound effect on every track. Automate volume and panning effects using the automation lanes in the Sequencer. Your soundtrack will be very effective if busses, trains, robots, and other sounds move across the speakers from side to side. You will get great results if you are patient and creative.

5. Check the level of every track so that it does not peak into the red zone. As you apply digital effects to each track, you will begin to tax the computer processor, because all digital effects are processed in real time, and the computer also has to process the video in real time. To help the computer do its job well (and not crash), you should freeze each sound effect track as you finish editing it. Use Track > Freeze Track or the shortcut key combination Ctrl+F to render the effect onto the track. You will hear the computer play the track and process it. Now that you've done this, the computer does not need to apply the track in real time, and it can save processor speed for other tasks. You can always unfreeze a track if you need to edit it later by using Track > Unfreeze Track or the shortcut key combination Ctrl+F. It is not possible to freeze the Video track.

6. Using your microphone and audio interface, record your narration/voices on a new Audio track. Remember to check the input source and recording level before you begin recording. It is wiser (though slower) to record the narration/voices in short sections than to do so in one long take. Remember to use Ctrl+I to trim the silence of each clip.

After the script is recorded, you can move the sections into the correct place on the timeline. The thumbnails on the Video track will help you line them up properly. You can place the sections of the narration/voices on separate Audio tracks. Use FX on the individual tracks if you want to make your voice(s) sound different.

7. Add some music to the beginning of the movie. You can use loops from the loop library, record sounds using Mixcraft's synthesizers (MinimogueVA, Impulse, Alien303), or record audio that you perform yourself. Think of the sort of music that you hear in Spider-Man, Batman, or Superman movies. Listen to some of the soundtracks of these movies by downloading them from iTunes or

searching for "Spider-Man soundtrack," "Batman soundtrack," or "Superman soundtrack" at www.youtube.com. Danny Elfman (the composer of the Spider-Man and Batman movies) and John Williams (the composer of the Superman movies) write music that is highly exciting, dramatic, and colorful. The Marvel comics that first contained these action heroes had these same traits, so the composers reflected that in their music.

8. Close the Video window and listen to your soundtrack with the Mixer window open. While you mix sounds for a video, it is a good practice to hide the Video window so you can concentrate on listening to how the sounds balance together. Make sure that levels are not peaking into the red and that the narration/voices can be heard at all times. Be prepared to cut the sounds of the music and effects so that the listener can hear the narration/voices clearly. You may need to unfreeze some tracks to adjust them. Remember to freeze them again after you have made adjustments. Have a friend listen to double-check that your mix is good.

9. Mix down your movie by selecting File > Mix Down To > AVI. You will now be able to watch the completed video on your computer using Windows Media Player or QuickTime. It would be fun to project the movie from the computer to a big screen using an LCD projector and play the soundtrack through the classroom speakers. Maybe your teacher will allow you to have a movie party where you can bring popcorn and dress up as characters from Marvel comics!

Extensions

Spider-Man: The Peril of Doc Ock was created by Tony Mines and Tim Drage, with music by Jason Graves. You will see their names in the credits at the end of the movie. You can see their work and hear their original soundtrack for this movie at www.spite-yourface.com. Their work is available at www.archive.org under the Creative Commons license, meaning they have made it available for you to download and watch. Try downloading one of Spite Your Face Productions' other projects from www.archive.org and add a new soundtrack. There's a very good *Star Wars: The Han Solo Affair* video that would be a great challenge to use for a soundtrack project. Also, check out other LEGO animations by going to www.brickfilms.com. You will need to convert any video to .avi or .wmv format to import it into Mixcraft. A very good free video converter is available at www.any-video-converter.com/products/for_video_free.

13 Working with Video in GarageBand

This chapter contains two lessons to help you learn to work with video in GarageBand. Please see the companion DVD for a written tutorial on working with video in GarageBand.

Lesson 1: Superman Sound Effects *by Michael Fein*

National Standards

2. Performing on instruments, alone and with others, a varied repertoire of music

4. Composing and arranging music within specified guidelines

6. Listening to, analyzing, and describing music

8. Understanding relationships between music, the other arts, and disciplines outside the arts

Objectives

- Add sound effects to the Superman movie clip.

- Use automation to mix the sound effects.

Class Time Required

You should be able to complete this lesson well in three one-hour sessions.

Materials

- Sound Effect entry at Wikipedia (en.wikipedia.org/wiki/Sound_effect)

- Superman Movie file located on companion DVD

- Event List Worksheet.pdf file located on companion DVD

- Superman SFX Template GarageBand file located on the companion DVD

Preparations

1. Read the Sound Effect entry at Wikipedia. Focus on the following topics:

   - The four main types of sound elements (hard sound effects, background sound effects, Foley sound effects, and design sound effects)

   - Sound effect techniques, including the use of various effect plug-ins (echo, flanger, phaser, chorus, and so on)

2. View the Superman Movie file in your QuickTime Player. Mute the volume for the video while viewing it.

3. Using the Event List Worksheet PDF file, complete the Event Description and Time columns. You will complete the Sound Used column in Step 4 of the "Procedure" section of this lesson.

Procedure

1. Open the file Superman SFX Template.band located on the companion DVD. This is a GarageBand file with Superman Movie already imported.

2. Open the Movie Preview window by clicking on the small preview window in the Movie track (see Figure 13.1).

Figure 13.1 Open the Movie Preview window by clicking on the small preview window in the Movie track.

Tip: You can resize the Movie Preview window and drag it to a new location on the screen.

---

3. Click on the Loop Browser and select the FX category.

4. Browse the various sound effects available and select one sound for each event you listed on the Event List Worksheet PDF in Step 3 of the "Preparations" section. Write the name of the sound effect on the worksheet.

Tip: To add additional sound effects into your file:

- Download free sound effects from the Internet. Check out www .partnersinrhyme.com for a large selection of free sound effects.

- Purchase a sound effects CD. I suggest searching "sound effects CD" at Amazon.com.

- Purchase individual sound effects files from the iTunes Store.
- Create your own sound effects using a microphone. Keep your ears open for the sound of objects around you. Try rattling keys, closing doors, crumpling paper, and so on and record these sounds into a new Basic track.

5. Drag the sound you selected for the first event into the gray area below the Movie track. GarageBand will create a new track for the sound effect. I suggest using Traffic Helicopter for the Robot Flying event. See Figure 13.2.

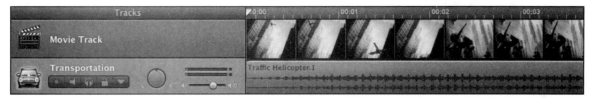

Figure 13.2 Import Traffic Helicopter for the first visual event.

6. Play the file. The sound should synchronize well with the video for the start of the Robot Flying event—*but* do you notice that the audio sound effect lasts too long?

7. Drag the play head to the left and right until you find the exact ending of the Robot Flying event.

Tip: Drag the zoom slider to the right to zoom in. This allows you to move the play head in smaller increments.

8. Place your cursor in the lower-right corner of the Traffic Helicopter region and trim the sound effect back to the red line of the play head (see Figure 13.3).

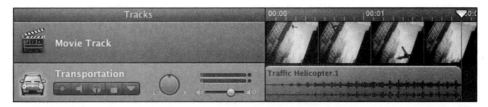

Figure 13.3 Trim the Traffic Helicopter region back to the red line of the play head.

9. Drag the sound you selected for the second event into the gray area to create another new track. I suggest using Tennis Serve for the Police Shooting event.

10. Drag the play head to the left and right until you find the exact beginning of the Police Shooting event.

11.   Drag the Tennis Serve region so it lines up exactly with the red line of the play head (see Figure 13.4).

Figure 13.4   Drag the Tennis Serve region so it lines up exactly with the red line of the play head.

12.   Play the file. The sound should synchronize well with the video for the start of the Police Shooting event—*but* do you notice that the audio sound effect is too short?

13.   Trim the Tennis Serve region shorter, as shown in Figure 13.5.

Figure 13.5   Trim the Tennis Serve region shorter.

14.   Drag the play head to the exact ending of the Police Shooting event, as shown in Figure 13.6.

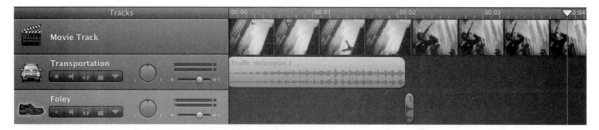

Figure 13.6   Drag the play head to the exact ending of the Police Shooting event.

15.   Place your cursor in the upper-right corner of the Tennis Serve region to display the Loop tool.

16.   Click and drag your cursor to the right and stop at the red line of the play head (see Figure 13.7).

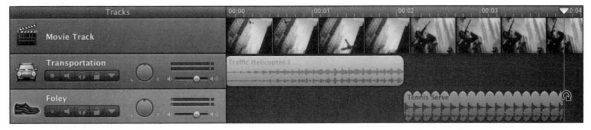

Figure 13.7   Loop the Tennis Serve region to the right and stop at the red line of the play head.

Tip: Try layering sounds to create a more realistic soundtrack; consider the four types of sound effects discussed in Step 1 of the "Preparations" section. For example, try adding Siren Sound Effect 02 to a new track below Tennis Serve, as shown in Figure 13.8. This provides a police siren sound (background sound effect) along with the shooting sound (hard sound effect).

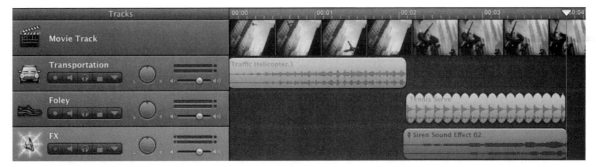

Figure 13.8   Add Siren Sound Effect 02 to a new track below Tennis Serve to add another sound-effect layer.

17.   Continue adding additional sound effects for every event. Remember to use the play head line as a guide for the beginning and ending of each event.

Tip: Sometimes the middle of a sound effect region should line up with an event. For example, I used Door Air Lock Closing for the Robot Landing event at 8.5 seconds. To sync this sound with the event, I placed my play head at the beginning of the event and then lined up the tallest sound wave from the Door Air Lock Closing sound with the red line from the play head. It is helpful to use the Track Editor window to see a more detailed view of the sound wave. See Figure 13.9.

Figure 13.9 Line up the tallest sound wave from the Door Air Lock Closing sound with the start of the Robot Landing event.

The final steps will walk you through mixing the sound effects tracks. First, you'll create a rough mix by setting the volume and panning of each track without any automation. Next, you'll create a final mix that includes volume and panning automation where appropriate.

18. Listen to the file and adjust the volume of each track appropriately. Sounds in the background should be softer than sounds in the foreground.

19. Listen to the file again and adjust the panning of each track appropriately. If a sound occurs on the left side of the video, pan it to the left. If a sound occurs on the right side of the video, pan it to the right.

20. Add volume automation. For example, for Robot Flying, it would be excellent to have the volume slowly increase as the robot gets closer, as shown in Figure 13.10.

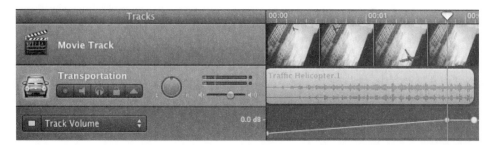

Figure 13.10 Fade in the volume of the Robot Flying event sound.

21. Add panning automation. For example, for Police Shooting, the guns move from right to left as they follow the robot flying, and it would be ideal to also pan the audio right to left for this event. See Figure 13.11.

Figure 13.11 Pan the Police Shooting event sound from right to left.

22. Play the file and evaluate the final product.
   - Is there a sound for every event?
   - Are all sounds in perfect synchronization with all visual events?
   - Did you set the volume for each sound effect appropriately?
   - Did you pan the sound effects appropriately?
   - Did you use volume and panning automation to bring life to your mix?

Extensions

Add effect plug-ins to various tracks to enhance the sound effect elements. See the Sound Effects entry at Wikipedia (as mentioned in the "Preparations" section) for more information and common techniques.

Compose a music soundtrack to accompany the sound effects. Use jingles or compose your own music using loops, MIDI keyboard, and/or acoustic instruments.

Tip: When adding music to a video, try to synchronize the music just as you would synchronize a sound effect. It is most effective to have a song begin at a significant action event or to line up a significant part of a song (such as the start of a chorus) with a significant action event.

Tip: Use the ducking feature to have the music automatically get softer when sound effects are playing. Turn on ducking by clicking Control > Ducking. Set the music tracks as secondary tracks with the ducking arrow down and set all sound effects tracks as primary tracks with the ducking arrow up.

Lesson 2: Atlas Collider Soundtrack *by Michael Fein*

National Standards

1. Singing, alone and with others, a varied repertoire of music

2. Performing on instruments, alone and with others, a varied repertoire of music

3. Improvising melodies, variations, and accompaniments

4. Composing and arranging music within specified guidelines

6. Listening to, analyzing, and describing music

7. Evaluating music and music performances

8. Understanding relationships between music, the other arts, and disciplines outside the arts

9. Understanding music in relation to history and culture

Objectives

- Compose an ambient music soundtrack for the Atlas Collider animation video.

Class Time Required

You should be able to complete this lesson well in three one-hour sessions.

Materials

- AmbientMusicGuide website (www.ambientmusicguide.com)

- Atlas Collider Template GarageBand file located on the companion DVD

- Atlas Collider Worksheet.pdf file located on the companion DVD

Preparations

1. Explore the AmbientMusicGuide website.

    a. Read History of Ambient (www.ambientmusicguide.com/pages/history.php).

    b. Explore the entries in A–Z Essential Releases and Key Artists (www.ambientmusicguide.com/pages/essential.php); preview some of these albums/artists using the iTunes Music Store.

    c. Listen to examples of ambient music by clicking Radio & Audio.

2. View the Atlas Collider Template. The video is essentially divided into five main sections.

    a. Introduction (see Figure 13.12)

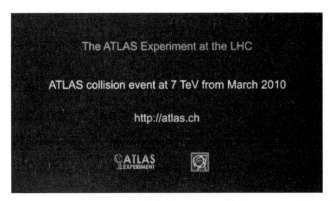

Figure 13.12 The Introduction scene of the ATLAS Collision movie.

b. Gray Tunnel (see Figure 13.13)

Figure 13.13 The Gray Tunnel scene of the ATLAS Collision movie.

c. Glowing Particles (see Figure 13.14)

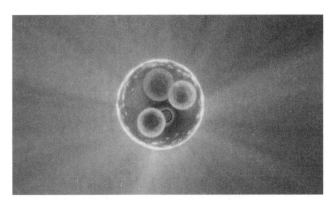

Figure 13.14 The Glowing Particles scene of the ATLAS Collision movie.

d. Blue Tunnel (see Figure 13.15)

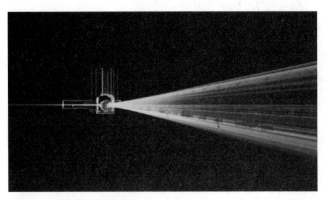

Figure 13.15 The Blue Tunnel scene of the ATLAS Collision movie.

e. Collision (see Figure 13.16)

Figure 13.16 The Collision scene of the ATLAS Collision movie.

Procedure

1. Open the Atlas Collider Template GarageBand file located on the companion DVD.

2. Open the Movie Preview window by clicking the preview window in the Movie track.

3. Play the file and make note of the start time of each main section. Notate this on the Atlas Collider Worksheet.

4. Create a new Software Instrument track. (Choose Track > New Track and then select Software Instrument.)

5. Select an instrument category and press some keys on your MIDI keyboard to audition the sound. I suggest trying out sounds in the following categories (although you can certainly use sounds in other categories):

   ■ Synth Basics
   ■ Synth Leads

- Synth Pads
- Synth Textures

Tip: If you don't have a MIDI keyboard, use GarageBand's virtual keyboard (Window > Musical Typing).

---

6. Select one primary instrument sound and one to three secondary instrument sounds for each section of the video. The primary sound will serve as the lead for the section and should be a sound that has a clear attack for each note. The secondary sounds will serve more as background and should be sounds that have a softer attack and a longer sustain. I suggest using Synth Leads for primary sounds and Synth Pads for secondary sounds. Notate your selections on the Atlas Collider Worksheet (see Figure 13.17).

7. In the Track Info pane, select the primary instrument sound for the introduction that you selected in the previous step.

8. Using only the black keys of the MIDI keyboard, compose a musical idea that will accompany the introduction. Remember, the goal is to have the musical idea represent the action in the video.

Tip: By using only black keys on the MIDI keyboard, you will be composing in E♭ Minor Pentatonic (E♭-G♭-A♭-B♭-D♭); see Figure 13.18.

---

9. Record the musical idea, as shown in Figure 13.19.

Tip: Record the primary sounds higher on the MIDI keyboard. Higher-pitched sounds will stand out more, and this is important for the primary sound.

Tip: Enable the count-in feature by selecting Control > Count In, as shown in Figure 13.20. This will provide a four-beat count-in before you begin recording. Under the Control menu, keep Metronome unchecked so you do not continue to hear the metronome after the count-in.

---

10. Create a new Software Instrument track.

11. In the Track Info pane, select the secondary instrument sound for the introduction that you selected in Step 6.

12. Again, using only black keys of the MIDI keyboard, compose a musical idea that will accompany your primary instrument recording.

Atlas Collider Worksheet

Event	Time	Primary Sound	Secondary Sound
Introduction		1.	1.
			2.
			3.
Gray Tunnel		1.	1.
			2.
			3.
Glowing Particles		1.	1.
			2.
			3.
Blue Tunnel		1.	1.
			2.
			3.
Collision		1.	1.
			2.
			3.

Figure 13.17   Atlas Collider Worksheet.pdf.

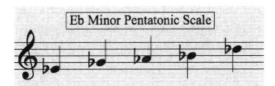

Figure 13.18   E♭ Minor Pentatonic scale.

Figure 13.19   Record the primary musical idea for the Introduction scene.

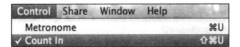

Figure 13.20   Select Control > Count In.

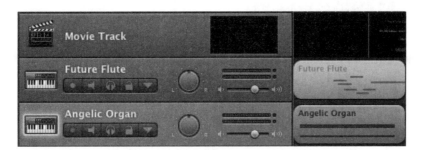

Figure 13.21   Record the secondary musical idea for the Introduction scene.

13.   Record this secondary musical idea, as shown in Figure 13.21.

Tip: Record the secondary sounds lower on the MIDI keyboard. Lower- or medium-pitched sounds will stand out less and serve as better background material.

---

14.   Repeat Steps 10 through 13 for any additional secondary instrument sounds for the introduction.

15.   Repeat Steps 7 through 14 for each section of the video.

Tip: When working on a section in the middle of the video, place your play head at the start of the section on which you are working. This will allow you to begin recording from this location instead of starting at the beginning of the file.

To enhance some action events, I recommend adding sound effects using your MIDI keyboard.

16.   Create a new Software Instrument track.

17.   In the Track Info pane, select Sound Effects and then select an instrument (see Figure 13.22). Each note on your MIDI keyboard will trigger a different sound effect.

Figure 13.22 Select an instrument sound from the Sound Effects category.

18.   Find an appropriate sound effect for a significant action in the video. For example, in the Nature Sounds instrument, press G#2 to get a thunder sound that would work well for the impact of the particles in the video.

Tip: You can also use sound effects as background material. For example, in the Nature Sounds instrument, press C3 to get an ocean sound that could be used during the Blue Tunnel section of the video.

---

19.   Record this sound effect.

20.   Evaluate your file.

- Do the musical ideas represent the visual elements in the video?
- Does each section have a clear primary musical element?
- Does each section have secondary musical elements that support the primary musical element?
- Do the sound effects enhance the actions in the video and synchronize perfectly?

Figure 13.23   The Atlas Experiment website (atlas.ch).

Extensions

Record an acoustic instrument into a new Basic track. You could use an acoustic instrument as a primary or secondary instrument. I recommend singing and then adding cool effect plug-ins, such as reverb, echo, and phaser.

Add sound effects for various action events in the video clip using sound effects in the Loop Browser. Open the Loop Browser and select the FX category. For example, add Booming Reverse 01 to enhance the visual impact of the particles.

Visit the Atlas Experiment website (www.atlas.ch) to find out more information about the scientific research being conducted at the Large Hadron Collider at CERN (see Figure 13.23). You will also find additional animation videos at this site (www.atlas.ch/multimedia/index-animation.html).

14 Multitrack Recording, Mixing, and Mastering in Mixcraft

This chapter contains two lessons to help you understand multitrack recording, mixing, and mastering in Mixcraft. Please see the companion DVD for a written tutorial on multitrack recording, mixing, and mastering in Mixcraft.

Lesson 1: You Think It's Easy? *by Richard McCready*

National Standards

4. Composing and arranging music within specified guidelines

6. Listening to, analyzing, and describing music

7. Evaluating music and music performances

Objectives

- Mix a multitrack song. (All the tracks on this song (except the violin) were played and recorded by Robin Hodson, one of the authors of this book.)

- Learn to manage the Mixer tab in Mixcraft effectively.

- Learn to use Send tracks.

- Learn to master the mix.

- Learn to make choices in creating a professional sound for your final mixdown.

Class Time Required

You should be able to complete this lesson well in three one-hour sessions.

Materials

- Computer with Mixcraft installed.

- Internet connection.

- Monitor speakers. The use of monitors rather than headphones is very important in mixing down audio to a professional standard.

- Raw data files from the companion DVD. Look in the Chapter 14 folder for a folder entitled You Think It's Easy. All the raw Audio tracks are contained in that folder.

■ You will find an MP3 of a completed mixdown of this project on the companion DVD. Look in the Chapter 14 folder for a file entitled You Think It's Easy Mixdown.mp3. You can also purchase the professionally mixed version from Robin Hodson's *The End of Days* album from Amazon.com—just search for "Robin Hodson music," and you will be able to download the song or the entire album.

Procedure

1. Launch Mixcraft and select the top option (Record Yourself or Your Band) from the New Project screen. Navigate to the You Think It's Easy folder and drag the first track (called You Think It's Easy – Track 01) onto the first Audio track in the Sequencer window. If you drag it over the left pane, where the Audio track's name is, the audio will snap to the beginning of the track.

   Drag each track in turn into the Sequencer window. When you get to the ninth track, you can drag it into the space below the other track names, and a new Audio track will be created for it. You can continue this with the tenth, eleventh, and twelfth tracks. Make sure all files are snapped to the beginning of the Sequencer window.

   Zoom in by rolling the mouse scroll wheel forward (or by using the + on the keyboard number pad) and see whether there are any gaps between the beginning of the timeline and the beginning of any Audio tracks. If there are, drag the tracks to the left until they are aligned with zero. Save your work and remember to keep saving every few minutes as you work.

2. Listen to the song. You will notice that you have some decisions to make. What will you do about the long silence before the track? Are the drums supposed to be in the music, or are they just in the mix to keep the musicians in time? What will you do about the long silence at the end?

3. Solo the first track. Click in the timeline above the first point at which you see audio in the track and press Play. What instrument do you hear? Press Stop. Click the track name at the left of the Audio track and type in the name of this instrument.

   Double-click the speaker icon under the track's new name and select a new icon for the track. Unsolo Track 1, solo Track 2, and listen to find out what instrument is on the track. You will notice that this instrument is the same instrument as Track 1. Do not delete it! There are two tracks of the same instrument in the mix—this is deliberate. You now need to label Track 1 and Track 2 so their names contain numbers. This means that if you think you heard a flute in Tracks 1 and 2, they should be labeled Flute 1 and Flute 2. (By the way, those are not flutes on those tracks—but you already knew that.)

Choose an icon for Track 2 by double-clicking the speaker icon. You will probably want to choose the same icon as for Track 1. Mixcraft does not give you a lot of choices.

4. Go through each track, soloing them and labeling them. You will find that some instruments are doubled—that means there are two recordings of the same instrument. Doubling is different from duplication. When you duplicate a track, you create an exact copy; when you double a track, you record it again with some slight changes to the sound or timing. Make sure you number each doubled instrument as you label it.

5. Right-click in the blank area below the name of each track (to the left of its Mute button). Select Color and choose a color for each track. You may like to color doubled instruments together. For example, you could choose the same color for both of the electric pianos. This will make it easier to locate your tracks as you mix.

   After you have colored all the tracks, you can rearrange them into whatever order you like by dragging each track up or down in the Sequencer. Click and hold the blank space under a track name (the same area you just right-clicked for color changing) and then drag the track up or down past one of the other tracks. You will see that you can move them all until you get them into an order you like.

   Keep like instruments together. Some studio musicians like to have their vocals at the top of the Sequencer window, whereas others like to have the bass and drums at the top—it is totally up to you.

6. Open the Mixer tab. Listen to the song and adjust the panning position for each instrument. You may want to imagine how they might sound on stage and place them so they come out of the speakers at those points. You will probably want to keep the vocals fairly near the center of the mix and fill out the rest of the space with different sounds.

   Place doubled instruments in different places in the mix. They are doubled for a reason—to give more presence to their sound. Think of how an orchestra has 30 violins or a rock band sometimes has three guitars. This is a standard multitracking technique, and you can achieve great sounds by mixing this way.

7. Solo the Vocal track. Use the simple EQ dials to shape the sound of the voice. Make sure the levels do not peak into the red zone as you add EQ. Unsolo the voice to hear how it sounds with the rest of the mix. Keep adjusting the EQ dials and the volume fader until you get a good sound.

   Repeat this step with every track on the Mixer. Use slightly different EQ settings for doubled instruments. It will take some time to work through every track, but do not hurry the job. It will be well worth it in the end.

If any tracks require more fine-tuning of their EQ or need compression, you can use the FX button to insert EQ or Compressor units. Try to avoid doing this for every track, or you will overly tax the computer's processor, and your audio could suffer as a result.

8.   Decide what to do with the drums. You can mute them or delete them entirely if you think they are unnecessary, or you can keep the volume fader on the drums quite low so they are not too dominant in the mix.

9.   Decide what to do with the silence at the beginning of the track. You could add another Audio track and use a microphone and audio interface to record your own introduction to the music, like a radio DJ announcing what the next song is. You could also cut the whole opening—select one track in the Sequencer window, choose Edit > Select All (shortcut key combination: Ctrl+A), right-click in the timeline just before the point where you want the music to start, select Split (shortcut key combination: Ctrl+T), delete the clips you do not want, and move all the tracks back to zero on the timeline. You will need to click somewhere off the tracks in the Sequencer to deselect everything.

10. Decide what to do with the end of the song. You will probably want to delete all of the unused audio at the end. Select all the tracks, split the tracks, and delete the unused portion, just like in Step 9. If you have decided to keep the drums in the mix, you will need to use the automation feature in the Sequencer to fade them out at the end of the song.

11. Return to the Mixer tab. Use Track > Add Track > Send Track to add a Send track to the mix. You will see it inserted between the last Audio track in your Mixer and the Master Mix fader. Double-click the name of the Send track and change it to Reverb. Click the FX button and add the Classic Reverb. Choose a preset you like.

12. You will now see that Send knobs have been added to all the tracks. Play the song and adjust the amount of signal that goes from each track into the reverb send by turning the Send knob. The amount of reverb that is sent from doubled instruments can remain the same—that is not a problem. Make sure the level in the Send track never goes into the red zone.

13. Add another Send track. Label it Chorus, add the Classic Chorus to the FX chain, and choose a preset. Mixcraft does not add another Send knob—you use the same one you used for the reverb channel, and Mixcraft remembers the level of the Send knob for each channel. Use the drop-down menu at the left of the Mixer tab to select Chorus as the send channel and send some of the audio from the tracks to the chorus.

You probably do not want to send chorus from every instrument. (Drums would be particularly strange with chorus.) With the doubled instruments, you should send different amounts to the chorus from each of them, or you could send one doubled instrument to the chorus send and not to the other. As you mix, you will see how effective that can be.

14. Just for fun, add the GSnap Pitch Correction to the FX chain on the Vocal track. Click Edit beside the preset selection column, and you will see the GSnap Pitch Correction Unit. Click Set Key and adjust the key of the unit to G minor. Now listen to what that does to the vocal. Pretty cool! You can keep that in your mix, if you like, or remove it—it's a matter of taste. Some people really like auto-tune; others hate it.

15. Click the FX button on the Master Mix fader. Add the Classic Master Limiter and select the Master CD preset. Press Edit beside the preset selection column so you can see the Classic Master Limiter unit. Listen to your song and adjust the Threshold knob to find a level in which your final mix sounds blended but not congested. You should be able to hear all the instruments well, but your mix should not feel as if all the instruments are trying to play as loudly as they can. Your Master Mix fader should almost hit the red zone but just fall short. This is a delicate process, but it is the final polishing touch that will make the mix sound as if it is on a professional CD, if you do it right.

16. Mix down your final version of "Do You Think It's Easy?" by selecting File > Mix Down To > MP3. Share your mix with your friends and family. We have already secured you permission from Robin Hodson (the composer and copyright holder) to post this mix online, so look ahead to Chapter 17, "Putting It All Together," for ideas on how to do this.

Extensions

If your processor can handle it, add new Send tracks and effects. Save your work as you go, just in case your computer crashes. It can be confusing at first to work out how sends operate; but once you get the hang of it, you'll become proficient very quickly. Try also adding the Shred Amp Simulator to the FX chain on the Guitar tracks—you can dial in some great guitar sounds with that.

Lesson 2: Susquehanna *by Richard McCready*

National Standards

4. Composing and arranging music within specified guidelines

6. Listening to, analyzing, and describing music

7. Evaluating music and music performances

Objectives

- Mix a 20-track song. (All the tracks on this song were played and recorded by Robin Hodson, one of the authors of this book.)

- Continue to develop skills in managing the Mixer tab in Mixcraft effectively.

- Learn how to automate Send tracks.

Class Time Required

You should be able to complete this lesson well in four one-hour sessions.

Materials

- Computer with Mixcraft installed.

- Internet connection.

- Monitor speakers. The use of monitors rather than headphones is very important in mixing down audio to a professional standard.

- Raw data files from the companion DVD. Look in the Chapter 14 folder for a folder entitled Susquehanna. All the raw Audio tracks are contained in that folder.

- You will find an MP3 of a completed mixdown of this project on the companion DVD. Look in the Chapter 14 folder for a file entitled Susquehanna Mixdown.mp3. You can also purchase the professionally mixed version from Robin Hodson's *The End of Days* album from Amazon.com—just search for "Robin Hodson music," and you will be able to download the song or the entire album.

Procedure

1. Launch Mixcraft and select the top option (Record Yourself or Your Band) from the New Project screen. Navigate to the Susquehanna folder and drag the first track (called Susquehanna – Track 01) onto the first Audio track in the Sequencer window. If you drag it over the left pane, where the Audio track's name is, the audio will snap to the beginning of the track.

    Drag each track in turn into the Sequencer window. When you get to the ninth track, you can drag it into the space below the other track names, and a new Audio track will be created for it. You can continue this with the rest of the tracks. Make sure all files are snapped to the beginning of the Sequencer window.

Zoom in by rolling the mouse scroll wheel forward (or by using the + on the keyboard number pad) and see whether there are any gaps between the beginning of the timeline and the beginning of any Audio tracks. If there are, drag the tracks to the left until they are aligned with zero. Save your work and remember to keep saving every few minutes as you work.

2. Listen to the song from the beginning until 6:30. At this point, there are just drums left on the tracks, so you don't need to listen to the rest—you'll be trimming that away. How many different instruments can you hear in the mix?

3. Solo the first track. Click in the timeline above the first point at which you see audio in the track and press Play. What instrument do you hear? Press Stop. Click the track name at the left of the Audio track and type in a name for this instrument.

    Double-click the speaker icon under the track's new name and select a new icon for the track. Unsolo Track 1, solo Track 2, and listen to find out what instrument is on the track. Label it and choose an icon. Go through all the tracks in turn, listening to them and labeling them. You may find that there are instruments you did not hear in the previous step. It will be your job as the studio engineer to make sure all these instruments are heard in the mix.

4. Right-click in the blank area below the name of each track (to the left of its Mute button). Select Color and choose a color for each track. You may like to color similar instruments the same. After you have colored all the tracks, you can rearrange them into whatever order you like by dragging each track up or down in the Sequencer. Click and hold the blank space under a track name (the same area you just right-clicked for color changing) and then drag the track up or down past one of the other tracks.

5. Open the Mixer tab. Listen to the song and adjust the panning position for each instrument. You may want to imagine how they might sound on stage and place them so they come out of the speakers at those points. You will probably want to keep the vocals fairly near the center of the mix and fill out the rest of the space with different sounds. Give careful consideration to instruments that are doubled.

6. Listen through the song several times and alter the levels of each instrument until you can hear them in the mix. You may find it helpful to use the simple EQ dials on the Mixer to highlight certain sounds and help them stand out in the mix.

7. Add a Send track and insert a reverb unit on it. Choose an appropriate preset for the song. Label the Send track as Reverb Send. Use the Send dials on the Mixer to send sounds from each track to the Reverb Send as you listen to the song.

8. You may find that you would like to automate how much reverb is being sent from each instrument to the Reverb Send. For example, the saxophone sounds good with plenty of reverb at the start of the song, but you would need to bring down this amount of reverb when the other instruments enter. You will be able to adjust the Reverb Send automation in the automation lane for the Saxophone track.

    In the Sequencer window, click on the Automation button in the Track Name pane. (It looks like a small line graph.) You will see that Track Volume is the default selection in the automation lane. Click the down arrow to the right of the words Track Volume and select Reverb. You can now add breakpoints to the automation line to control the amount of send from the track. Give the saxophone plenty of reverb at the start of the song and then bring down that level by drawing in breakpoints later in the track. Solo the Saxophone track and listen to it to hear that effect work. Listen again with all the instruments playing. You can adjust the breakpoints as you listen.

9. Create another Send track and label it Drum Compressor. There are a lot of Drum tracks in this song, so it would be good to compress them together in one Send track in order to keep the sound smooth. Choose a good preset for drums and change the Send Channel selector in the Mixer to Drum Compressor. Solo all the Drum tracks and adjust the amount of sound going into the Send track from the Send knobs until you have a smooth drum sound. Listen to the drums together and also listen to them with the rest of the mix.

10. Check the levels of every track to make sure that you can still hear all the sounds and that they are well balanced. Add compressors and/or EQs to some tracks to highlight those sounds.

11. Continue to check levels of each sound as you mix. Make sure levels do not go into the red zone on the channel strips in the Mixer.

12. Listen to the end of the song (around 6:00–6:30 on the timeline) and find a point at which you would like the mix to fade out. Use Track > Show Master Track to bring up the master fader in the Sequencer. Use the automation lane to create a slow fade at the end of the song. Use Edit > Select All (or the shortcut key combination Ctrl+A) to select all the tracks in the Sequencer. Right-click on one of the tracks just after the end of the fade and select Split from the drop-down menu. Click in a blank space in the Sequencer window to deselect everything and then delete the unused region from each track. (Select each clip after the split point by clicking on its name bar and pressing Delete.)

13. Check your song several times to make sure everything is correct. Add the Classic Master Limiter to the Main Mix Fader FX chain and select the Master CD preset. Mix down your final version of "Susquehanna" by selecting

File > Mix Down To > MP3. Share your mix with your friends and your family. We have already secured you permission from Robin Hodson (the composer and copyright holder) to post this mix online, so look ahead to Chapter 17 for ideas on how to do this.

Extensions

You should now be able to mix other songs. Find out whether any of your friends are in bands and ask them whether they have some raw audio that you could mix for them. You can also search the Internet for unmixed audio that you can use to hone your skills. These unmixed Audio tracks are usually called *stems*, and several artists have released sets of stems on the Internet that you can download freely and use for mixing. Use Google or another search engine to look for Radiohead, Nine Inch Nails, or Peter Gabriel stems or visit www.remixstems.com. Also, look ahead to Chapter 16, "Putting It All Together: Two Final Projects for Mixcraft or GarageBand," for a remix project using Nine Inch Nails stems.

15 Multitrack Recording, Mixing, and Mastering in GarageBand

This chapter contains two lessons to help you understand multitrack recording, mixing and mastering in GarageBand. Please see the companion DVD for a written tutorial on multitrack recording, mixing, and mastering in GarageBand.

Lesson 1: Multitrack Drum Mix *by Michael Fein*

National Standards

2. Performing on instruments, alone and with others, a varied repertoire of music

3. Improvising melodies, variations, and accompaniments

4. Composing and arranging music within specified guidelines

6. Listening to, analyzing, and describing music

7. Evaluating music and music performances

Objectives

- Mix the drum recording by adjusting volume and panning of each track.

- Mix the drum recording by applying EQ and reverb effect plug-ins to each track.

- Use a compressor effect plug-in on the Master Track.

Class Time Required

You should be able to complete this lesson well in three one-hour sessions.

Materials

- "Recording and Mixing Drums" by Bob Dennis, available online at www.recordingeq.com/EQ/req0301/feature.html

- Drum Mixing Template.band GarageBand file located on companion DVD

Preparations

1. Listen to a variety of rock-and-roll recordings and focus on the drums in each song. I suggest listening to songs from the following albums: Bon Jovi's *Slippery*

When Wet and Maroon 5's *Songs About Jane*. Students can also bring in their favorite albums and listen to them with a focus on the drums.

2. Read "Recording and Mixing Drums" by Bob Dennis. This article describes microphone placement as well as mixing/processing.

Note: Mixing is a subjective art. The procedures in this lesson are a guide to help you mix this file. It is a good idea to use the suggested settings and then experiment to see whether you prefer slightly (or drastically) different settings. It is through this experimentation that you will really start to learn how to mix.

Procedure

1. Locate the file Drum Mixing Template.band on the companion DVD and copy it to your computer's hard drive.

2. Open Drum Mixing Template.band in GarageBand and listen to the file.

3. Solo the Kick track.

4. Open the Track Info pane and be sure that you have the Kick track selected.

5. Click the Edit tab in the Track Info pane.

6. Click on an empty box in this window and add the Track Reverb effect plug-in.

7. Click on the effect plug-in icon to open the detailed effect plug-in settings window, as shown in Figure 15.1.

Figure 15.1 Click on the Track Reverb icon to open the settings window.

8. Adjust the settings of the Track Reverb effect plug-in as follows (see Figure 15.2):

    ■ Reverb Time: 8%

    ■ Reverb Color: −7%

    ■ Reverb Volume: 15%

    ■ Original Volume: 85%

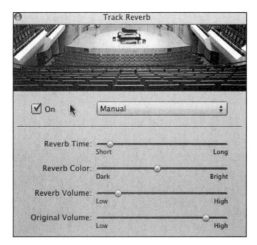

Figure 15.2 Settings for a short reverb.

9. Click the preset pop-up window that currently says Manual.

10. Click on Make Preset, as shown in Figure 15.3.

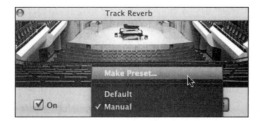

Figure 15.3 Select Make Preset and save as Drums – Short Reverb.

11. Name the preset Drums – Short Reverb and click Save. You can now access this preset for other Drum tracks in this file.

12. Close the Track Reverb settings window.

13. Enable the Visual EQ effect plug-in near the bottom of the Track Info window by clicking the gray square. (It will turn blue when enabled.) See Figure 15.4.

Figure 15.4 Enable the Visual EQ effect plug-in.

14. Click on the Visual EQ icon to open the detailed effect plug-in settings window.

15. Click on Details at the bottom of the effect plug-in settings window.

16. Click your cursor in the Bass section of this window. Drag left and right until the frequency is set to 78.0 Hz and drag up and down until the volume is set to +9.0 dB.

17. Click your cursor in the Low Mid section of this window. Drag left and right until the frequency is set to 445 Hz and drag up and down until the volume is set to −6.5 dB.

18. Click your cursor in the High Mid section of this window. Drag left and right until the frequency is set to 4,000 Hz and drag up and down until the volume is set to +6.5 dB.

Tip: You can also enter EQ settings by double-clicking any value in the Details section of the Visual EQ effect settings window (see Figure 15.5).

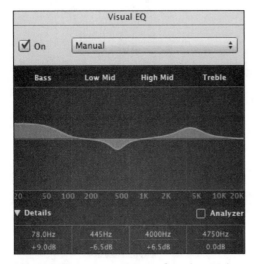

Figure 15.5 EQ settings for the Kick track.

---

19. Close the Visual EQ settings window.

20. Un-solo the Kick track.

21. Select the Snare track, solo the track, and listen to the file.

22. Add a Track Reverb effect plug-in and open the detailed settings window.

23. Adjust the settings of the Track Reverb effect plug-in as follows (see Figure 15.6):
    - Reverb Time: 18%
    - Reverb Color: −7%
    - Reverb Volume: 15%
    - Original Volume: 85%

24. Click the preset pop-up window and select Make Preset.

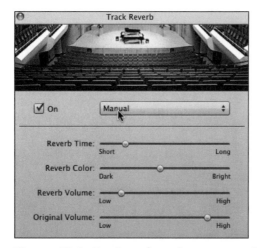

Figure 15.6 Settings for a longer reverb.

25. Name the preset Drums – Long Reverb and click Save.

26. Close the Track Reverb settings window.

27. Enable the Visual EQ effect plug-in and open the detailed settings window.

28. Click your cursor in the High Mid section of this window. Drag left and right until the frequency is set to 4600 Hz and drag up and down until the volume is set to +5.5 dB. See Figure 15.7.

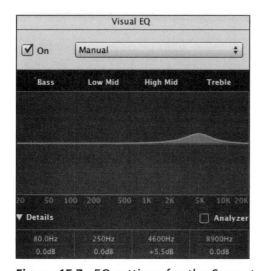

Figure 15.7 EQ settings for the Snare track.

29. Solo the Kick and Snare tracks.

30. Adjust the volume of the Snare track all the way down.

31. Play the file and slowly turn up the volume of the Snare track to create a good blend between the Kick and Snare tracks. Note that both tracks should be panned center.

32. Un-solo the Kick and Snare tracks.

33. Select the Hi-Hat track, solo the track, and listen to the file.

34. Add a Track Reverb effect plug-in and open the detailed settings window.

35. Click the preset pop-up window and select Drums – Short Reverb. This is the preset that you created in Step 11.

36. Enable the Visual EQ effect plug-in and open the detailed settings window.

37. Click your cursor in the Bass section of this window. Drag left and right until the frequency is set to 215 Hz and drag up and down until the volume is set to −6.5 dB.

38. Click your cursor in the Treble section of this window. Drag left and right until the frequency is set to 10,800 Hz and drag up and down until the volume is set at +5.5 dB. See Figure 15.8.

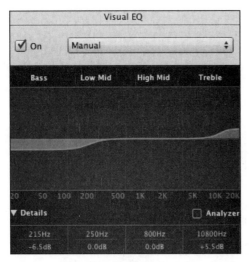

Figure 15.8 EQ settings for the Hi-Hat track.

39. Solo the Kick, Snare, and Hi-Hat tracks.

40. Adjust the volume of the Hi-Hat track all the way down.

41. Pan the Hi-Hat track all the way to the left (which is also known as *hard left*). Note: I prefer to mix the drums from the drummer's perspective, so I place the Hi-Hat track on the right side of the mix as if I were sitting on the drummer's stool.

42. Play the file and slowly turn up the volume of the Hi-Hat track to create a good blend between the three tracks. Keep an eye on the master level meter located in the bottom toolbar. You want to turn up the Hi-Hat track until the left channel

jumps up just a bit more than the right channel. Note that the left channel is the top level meter and the right channel is the bottom level meter. See Figure 15.9.

Figure 15.9 Panning and volume settings for the Kick, Snare, and Hi-Hat tracks.

43. Un-solo the Kick, Snare, and Hi-Hat tracks.

44. Select the Rack Tom track, solo the track, and listen to the file.

45. Add a Track Reverb effect plug-in and open the detailed settings window.

46. Click the preset popup window and select Drums – Long Reverb. This is the preset that you created in Step 25.

47. Enable the Visual EQ effect plug-in and open the detailed settings window.

48. Click your cursor in the Bass section of this window. Drag left and right until the frequency is set to 81.0 Hz and drag up and down until the volume is set to +9.0 dB.

49. Click your cursor in the Low Mid section of this window. Drag left and right until the frequency is set to 400 Hz and drag up and down until the volume is set to −6.0 dB.

50. Click your cursor in the High Mid section of this window. Drag left and right until the frequency is set to 7000 Hz and drag up and down until the volume is set to +4.0 dB. See Figure 15.10.

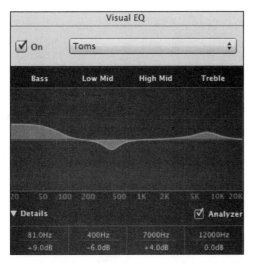

Figure 15.10 EQ settings for the Rack Tom track.

51. Select the Floor Tom track, solo the track, and listen to the file.

52. Add a Track Reverb effect plug-in and open the detailed settings window.

53. Click the preset pop-up window and select Drums – Long Reverb. This is the preset that you created in Step 25.

54. Enable the Visual EQ effect plug-in and open the detailed settings window.

55. Click your cursor in the Bass section of this window. Drag left and right until the frequency is set to 94.0 Hz and drag up and down until the volume is set to +7.0 dB.

56. Click your cursor in the Low Mid section of this window. Drag left and right until the frequency is set to 400 Hz and drag up and down until the volume is set to −9.5 dB.

57. Click your cursor in the High Mid section of this window. Drag left and right until the frequency is set to 4600 Hz and drag up and down until the volume is set to +6.0 dB. See Figure 15.11.

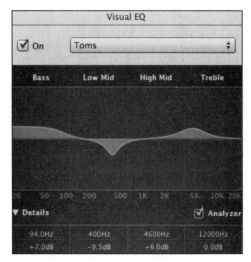

Figure 15.11 EQ settings for the Floor Tom track.

58. Un-solo all tracks and mute the Overhead Right and Overhead Left tracks.

59. Pan the Rack Tom track left center and the Floor Tom track right center.

60. Cycle a section of the song that includes rack and floor tom hits.

61. Play the file and adjust the volume of both Tom tracks to create a good balance between the tracks. See Figure 15.12.

62. Select the Overhead Right track, solo the track, and listen to the file.

Figure 15.12 Volume and panning settings for the Tom tracks.

63. Pan the Overhead Right track hard right.

64. Add a Track Reverb effect plug-in and open the detailed settings window.

65. Click the preset pop-up window and select Drums – Short Reverb. This is the preset that you created in Step 25.

66. Enable the Visual EQ effect plug-in and open the detailed settings window.

67. Click your cursor in the Bass section of this window. Drag left and right until the frequency is set to 210.0 Hz and drag up and down until the volume is set to −6.5 dB.

68. Click your cursor in the Treble section of this window. Drag left and right until the frequency is set to 10,000 Hz and drag up and down until the volume is set to +4.5 dB. See Figure 15.13.

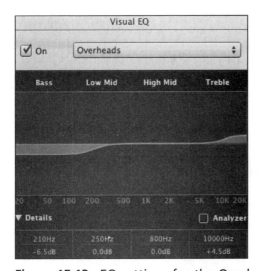

Figure 15.13 EQ settings for the Overhead tracks.

69. Select the Overhead Left track, solo the track, and listen to the file.

70. Pan the Overhead Left track hard left.

71. Repeat Steps 64 to 68 using the Overhead Left track.

72. Unsolo the Overhead tracks.

73. Play the file and adjust the volume of the Overhead tracks. As you adjust the volume, listen closely for the crash cymbal in the Overhead Left track and the

ride cymbal in the Overhead Right track. Bring up the volume until you hear just enough cymbals.

74. Select Master Track located near the top of the Track Info pane, as shown in Figure 15.14.

Figure 15.14 Select Master Track in the Track Info pane.

75. Click on the Edit tab in the Track Info pane.

76. Click in the empty effects box and select AUDynamicsProcessor.

Tip: A dynamics processor is the same as a compressor or a limiter. These effects reduce the volume of the loudest sound waves and allow you to make your entire file feel louder.

---

77. Play the file and begin to adjust the threshold by clicking and dragging the yellow node up and down the curved line. As the file plays, an arrow will indicate the input volume of the file. As the arrow exceeds your threshold setting, it will turn red; this means that the sound is being reduced or compressed. You want the threshold set so only the loudest sounds are reduced. I suggest setting the threshold to about −33.1 dB for this file. See Figure 15.15.

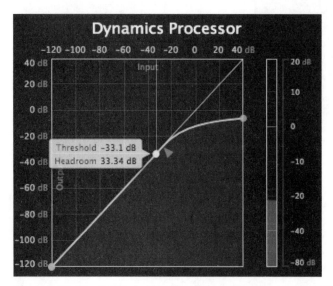

Figure 15.15 Settings for the Dynamics Processor effect plug-in on the Master Track.

78.   Click the Details arrow in the effect window.

79.   Adjust the attack time. If the attack time is set too low, you may hear an unnatural pulsing sort of sound in the Drum track. If the attack time is set too high, it will take too long to compress the loudest sound waves. I suggest setting the attack to about 0.015 seconds.

80.   Adjust the release time. If the release is set too low, you may again hear an unnatural pulsing sort of sound. If the release is set too high, it will continue to compress the sound long after the loud sound wave has passed. I suggest setting the release to about 0.2 seconds.

81.   Adjust the master gain setting. As you increase the master gain, keep an eye on the Output Level meter located in the AUDynamicsProcessor effect window. If you set the master gain too high, you can cause clipping and distorted sound. Slowly increase the master gain until the Output Level meter hits just below 0 dB. I suggest setting the master gain to 5.0 dB for this file.

82.   Export the finished mix by selecting Share > Send Song to iTunes or Share > Export Song to Disk.

83.   If you plan to burn this finished file to an audio CD, uncheck Compress in the Export window. This will export the final mix as a full CD-quality file. If you plan to post the file to a website or add it to your iPod, check Compress. A compressed file is great for the Internet or an iPod because it is significantly smaller (about 1/10th the size of a CD-quality file); however, you lose a small bit of quality. The most common compressed audio files are MP3 and AAC files.

Extensions

Create Software Instrument tracks and compose/record new melodic and harmonic material to accompany the drums using the MIDI keyboard.

Create new Basic tracks and compose/record new melodic and harmonic material to accompany the drums using acoustic instruments or your voice.

Special thanks to Emanuel DelPizzo for generously donating his time to perform on drums for this recording. Visit Mr. DelPizzo's website at www.wetpaintaudio.com.

Lesson 2: Train Song Mix *by Michael Fein*

National Standards

6. Listening to, analyzing, and describing music

7. Evaluating music and music performances

8. Understanding relationships between music, the other arts, and disciplines outside the arts.

Objectives

- Mix a large multitrack recording using effect plug-ins and volume/panning adjustments.

- Explore Guitar tracks in GarageBand.

Class Time Required

You should be able to complete this lesson well in three one-hour sessions.

Materials

- Train Song – M Fein Mix.mp3 audio file located on the companion DVD

- Train Song Template.band GarageBand file located on the companion DVD

Preparations

1. Listen to a variety of rock-and-roll recordings. Focus on the mix. I suggest listening to AC/DC's *Back in Black*.

   - Listen closely for each individual instrument and consider the panning.

   - Listen for the amount of reverb on the recording.

   - Listen for any interesting effect plug-ins that may have been used on various instruments. This would include distortion/overdrive on Guitar tracks.

2. Listen to Train Song – M Fein Mix.mp3, located on the companion DVD. This is my final mixed version of "Train Song" after completing all of the procedures below.

Note: There are a million ways to mix this file. I encourage you to try the procedures in this chapter and use them as a guide, but please feel free to *experiment* as you mix. Remember, you can always undo, and it often pays to be adventurous.

Procedure

1. Locate Train Song Template.band, located on the companion DVD and copy it to your computer's hard drive.

2. Open Train Song Template.band in GarageBand.

3. Listen to the file. As the file plays, solo each track to get a feel for the audio on each track. You may notice that during the drum intro in the beginning of the song, you can hear background noise on the other tracks.

4. Press Command+A to select all of the regions.

5. Press and hold Shift and click the audio region in the Kick Snare track to deselect it.

6. Use the Trim tool to remove the silence from all regions except the Kick Snare region. Trim to about Bar 2 Beat 4 when the sound waves begin (see Figure 15.16).

Figure 15.16 Trim all regions except Kick Snare to Bar 2 Beat 4.

Tip: It is advisable to trim out any large area of silence on any track to avoid distracting background noise. If there is a long section of silence in the middle of a track, split the region and then trim the silence.

Let's focus on the Vocal tracks first.

7. Solo the three Vocal tracks.

8. Drag the play head to Bar 11 and listen to the Vocal tracks.

9. Select the Lead Vocals track and open the Track Info pane.

10. Click the Edit tab in the Track Info pane.

11. Enable the Compressor effect plug-in by clicking the gray square next to the plug-in icon.

12. Click on the word Manual and select Vocal Compression Basic from the preset list (see Figure 15.17). The compressor will reduce the amplitude of the loudest sound waves and enable you to make the track feel louder in the mix.

Figure 15.17 Select the Vocal Compression Basic preset in the Compressor effect plug-in.

13. Select an empty effect plug-in box and add Track Reverb.

14. Click the word Default and select Vocal Room from the preset list, as shown in Figure 15.18.

Figure 15.18 Select the Vocal Room preset in the Track Reverb effect plug-in.

15. Select the Backing Vocals 1 track.

16. Enable the Compressor effect plug-in and select Vocal Compression Basic from the preset list.

17. Add Track Reverb and select Vocal Hall from the preset list, as shown in Figure 15.19. Note that some engineers would prefer that all Vocal tracks have identical reverb; however, I like the sound of using slightly different, more distant reverb for the backing vocals in this particular file.

Figure 15.19 Select the Vocal Hall preset in the Track Reverb effect plug-in.

18. Pan the Backing Vocals 1 track slightly left (−29) and the Backing Vocals 2 track slightly right (+37). This will provide some stereo separation for the Vocal tracks. Keep the Lead Vocals panned center.

19. Reduce the volume of the Backing Vocal tracks so they are slightly softer than the Lead Vocals. In my mix, I set the Backing Vocals to −8.8 dB and the Lead Vocals to −4.8 dB. See Figure 15.20.

Figure 15.20 Volume and panning levels for the Vocal tracks.

20. Un-solo the Vocal tracks and close all effect plug-in setting windows.

21. Next, focus on the Bass track. Select and solo the Bass track.

22. Listen to the Bass track.

23. In the Track Info pane, select the Bass category.

24. Play the file. While the file plays, try out various bass settings from the Track Info pane. I suggest using Studio Direct Box Warm for a nice deep bass tone with less attack (see Figure 15.21).

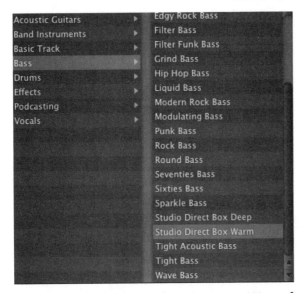

Figure 15.21 Select Studio Direct Box Warm from the Bass category.

25. Solo the Vocal tracks along with the Bass track.

26. Listen to the file and adjust the volume of the Bass track so it blends well with the Vocal tracks. In my mix, I set the Bass to −4.8 dB. See Figure 15.22.

Figure 15.22 Volume and panning settings for the Vocal and Bass tracks.

27. Un-solo all tracks and close all effect plug-in setting windows.

28. Next, focus on the Drum tracks. Solo the Kick Snare and Crash tracks.

29. Listen to the two tracks together.

30. Select the Kick Snare track.

31. In the Track Info pane, select the Drums category and then select Thickened Drums from the list on the right, as shown in Figure 15.23.

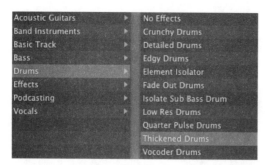

Figure 15.23 Select Thickened Drums from the Drums category.

32. Click on the Edit tab and click on the Compressor icon.

33. Select Drum Kit Punchy from the preset pop-up menu, as shown in Figure 15.24.

Figure 15.24 Select Drum Kit Punchy from the preset menu in the Compressor effect plug-in.

34. Drag the Gain slider to the right to 13.5 dB, as shown in Figure 15.25. This will increase the volume of the Kick Snare track. You will rarely increase gain by this huge amount, but in this case the Drum track was recorded with very low levels. Note that when you adjust the Gain slider, the preset will change to Manual.

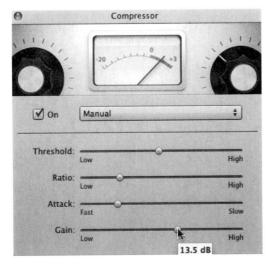

Figure 15.25 Increase the gain in the Compressor to 13.5 dB for the Kick Snare track.

35.   Select the Crash track.

36.   In the Track Info pane, click the Edit tab.

37.   Enable the Compressor effect plug-in and click on the plug-in icon to open the settings window.

38.   Drag the Gain slider to the right to about 10 dB, as shown in Figure 15.26.

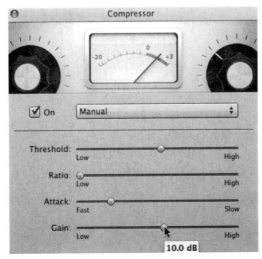

Figure 15.26 Set the gain in the Compressor to 10 dB for the Crash track.

39.   Pan the Crash track slightly to the right (+24), as shown in Figure 15.27.

Figure 15.27 Pan the Crash track slightly to the right.

40.   Solo the Vocal, Bass, and Drum tracks.

41.   Listen to the file and adjust the volume of the Drum tracks appropriately. I ended up leaving the Drum volumes at 0.0 dB.

42.   Un-solo all tracks and close all effect plug-in setting windows.

43.   Next, focus on the Guitar Rhythm tracks. Select and solo the Guitar Rhythm 1 track.

44.   Listen to the track.

45.   In the Track Info pane, select the Edit tab.

46.   Enable the Visual EQ effect plug-in.

47.   Click the word Manual and select Guitar Brighten from the pop-up menu, as shown in Figure 15.28. This will increase the frequencies around 5600 Hz by 6.5 dB.

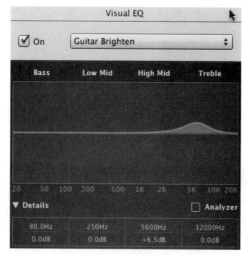

Figure 15.28 Select Guitar Brighten from the preset menu in the Visual EQ effect plug-in.

48.   Repeat Steps 42 through 46 on the Guitar Rhythm 2 track.

49.   Solo both Guitar Rhythm tracks.

50.   Pan Guitar Rhythm 1 hard left (−64) and Guitar Rhythm 2 hard right (+64), as shown in Figure 15.29.

Figure 15.29 Pan the Guitar Rhythm 1 track hard left and the Guitar Rhythm 2 track hard right.

51.   Solo the Vocal, Bass, Drum, and Guitar Rhythm tracks.

52.   Listen to the file and adjust the volume of the Guitar Rhythm tracks appropriately. I suggest letting the Guitar Rhythm tracks sit fairly prominent in the mix because these tracks really provide a lot of drive to the tune. I set the volume of both Guitar Rhythm tracks to about −3.8 dB.

Next, focus on the Guitar Fills tracks. These tracks contain electric guitar recorded direct (meaning no amplifier was used during the recording; a cable ran from the guitar's output directly to the recording interface). GarageBand now includes a host of amp modeling effects that will liven up the sound of the stale-sounding electric guitar fills.

53.   Select Track > New Track and choose Electric Guitar from the pop-up window, as shown in Figure 15.30.

Figure 15.30   Create a new Electric Guitar track.

54.   Drag this track up so it is directly below the Guitar Fills 1 track.

Tip: Be sure Show Alignment Guides is selected under the Control menu. This will allow you to drag the region to another track without moving it left or right. Even a subtle change in the positioning of the region on the timeline will really throw off the timing of the track.

---

55.   Drag the audio region from Guitar Fills 1 to the new Electric Guitar track that you created in Step 53 (see Figure 15.31).

Figure 15.31   Drag the audio region from Guitar Fills 1 to the new Electric Guitar track.

56.   Solo the new track and play the file.

57.   As the file plays, audition various amplifier models by pressing the arrow icons next to the amplifier image in the Track Info pane. I selected the Backface

Combo, as shown in Figure 15.32. Note: The effect setting is called Clean Combo, and the name of the amplifier pictured is Backface Combo.

Figure 15.32 Select Backface Combo from the amplifier choices.

Tip: Find out the name of the amplifier and some information about it by hovering your cursor on top of the amplifier image.

---

58. Press Command+D to duplicate this Electric Guitar track.

59. Drag the audio region from Guitar Fills 2 to the duplicate Electric Guitar track.

60. Delete the old Guitar Fills tracks (press Command+Delete).

61. Rename the new Electric Guitar tracks as Guitar Fills 1 AMP and Guitar Fills 2 AMP.

62. Solo the Guitar Fills AMP tracks.

63. Pan Guitar Fills 1 AMP hard left (−64) and Guitar Fills 2 AMP hard right (+63), as shown in Figure 15.33.

Figure 15.33 Pan the Guitar Fills AMP tracks hard left and hard right.

64. Solo the Vocal, Bass, Drum, Guitar Rhythm, and Guitar Fills AMP tracks.

65. Listen to the file and adjust the volume of the Guitar Fills AMP tracks appropriately. I set the volume of both Guitar Fills AMP tracks to −4.8 dB.

66. Un-solo all tracks.

67. Next, focus on the Guitar Distortion track. Create a new Electric Guitar track (Track > New Track and select Electric Guitar).

68. Drag this track directly under the Guitar Distortion track.

69. Drag the region from Guitar Distortion to the new Electric Guitar track, as shown in Figure 15.34.

Figure 15.34 Drag the region from Guitar Distortion to the new Electric Guitar track.

70. Delete the old Guitar Distortion track.

71. Click the pop-up window above the amplifier image.

72. Play the file and audition various amplifier and stomp-box preset combinations. Solo and un-solo the track as it plays to see how this track fits with the other tracks. I suggest using Liverpool Bright, as shown in Figure 15.35.

Figure 15.35 Select Liverpool Bright from the preset menu in the Track Info pane.

73. Click the amplifier image to open and view the amplifier settings. Reduce the Presence knob (see Figure 15.36).

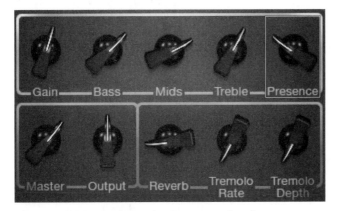

Figure 15.36 Reduce the Presence knob.

74. Click the Edit button above the amplifier image.

75. Click the Sustain stomp-box. This will reveal the 10 stomp-box effects available in GarageBand. **GarageBand '11 users note:** You have 15 stomp-box effects available.

76. Drag the Retro Chorus stomp-box to an empty yellow box above, as shown in Figure 15.37.

Figure 15.37 Drag Retro Chorus to an empty yellow box.

Tip: Double-click the Chorus stomp-box to open the settings window below. These effects work identically to a real guitar stomp-box. Press the foot pedal at the bottom of the effect to enable or disable it (a red light goes on when the effect is enabled) and adjust the knobs to modify the sound (see Figure 15.38).

Figure 15.38 Adjust the knobs of the Retro Chorus stomp-box.

---

77. Mute the Slide Guitar and Harmonica tracks. Note that it makes more sense to mute the two tracks we haven't worked with yet than to solo the huge number of tracks that we have already mixed.

78. Listen to the file and adjust the volume of the Guitar Distortion track appropriately. I suggest burying this track in the mix so it only provides a bit of texture to the mix. I set the volume of this track to −16.9 dB.

79. Un-mute all tracks.

80. Next, focus on the Slide Guitar track. Select and solo the Slide Guitar track.

81. Click the Edit tab in the Track Info pane.

82. Enable the Compressor effect plug-in and click on the icon to open the settings window.

83. Increase the Gain slider to about 5.5 dB, as shown in Figure 15.39.

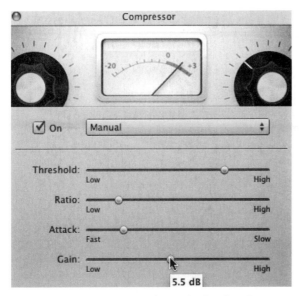

Figure 15.39 Increase the gain in the Compressor to 5.5 dB.

84. Pan the Slide Guitar track slightly right (+25).

85. Mute the Harmonica track and un-solo the Slide Guitar track.

86. Play the file and adjust the volume of the Slide Guitar appropriately. I suggest letting the Slide Guitar sit prominently in the mix because it adds so much character to the song. I set the volume to about −1.6 dB (see Figure 15.40).

Figure 15.40 Volume and panning settings for the Slide Guitar track.

87. Next, focus on the Harmonica track. Select and solo the Harmonica track.

88. Click the Edit tab in the Track Info pane.

89. Enable the Visual EQ effect plug-in and click the icon to open the settings window.

90. Reduce the upper High Mid frequencies by 3 dB to help it fit better in the mix (see Figure 15.41).

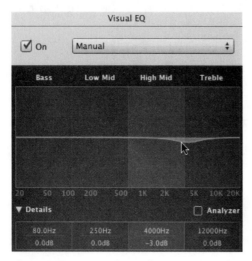

Figure 15.41 Reduce the upper High Mid frequencies by 3 dB.

91. Pan the Harmonic track slightly left (−27).

92. Un-solo the Harmonica track and listen to the file.

93. Set the volume of the Harmonica track appropriately. I set the volume to −5.6dB.

94. Open the volume automation lane for the Harmonica track.

95. Reduce the volume of the Harmonica at Bar 34 to about −7.9 dB, as shown in Figure 15.42. This will keep the Harmonica out of the way of the vocals throughout the rest of the song.

Figure 15.42 Automate the volume of the Harmonic track softer at Bar 34.

96. Finally, we will focus on the Master Track. Select Track > Show Master Track.

97.   Select the Master Track at the bottom of the screen.

98.   In the Track Info pane, select the Rock category and then select Rock Refreshing Sparkle, as shown in Figure 15.43.

Figure 15.43 Select Rock Refreshing Sparkle from the Rock category on the Master Track.

99.   Click the Edit tab.

100.   Disable the Echo and Reverb effect plug-ins, as shown in Figure 15.44.

Figure 15.44 Disable Echo and Reverb on the Master Track.

101.   Click the Visual EQ icon to open the settings window.

102.   Bring the Treble frequencies up about 2.0 dB at about 12,000 Hz and bring the Bass frequencies up about 3.0 dB at about 80 Hz by clicking and dragging on the graph (see Figure 15.45).

103.   Close the effect settings window.

104.   Under the Compressor effect plug-in, click the words Rock Basic and select Rock Punch from the pop-up window, as shown in Figure 15.46.

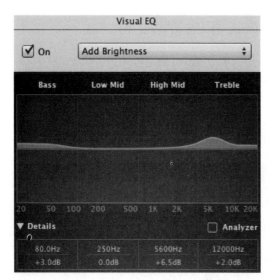

Figure 15.45 EQ settings for the Master Track.

Figure 15.46 Select the Rock Punch preset in the Compressor on the Master Track.

105. Create a fade-out in the Master Track using automation on the Master Volume line. Begin the fade at Bar 117 and end the fade at Bar 121, as shown in Figure 15.47.

Figure 15.47 Fade out the Master Volume starting at Bar 117 and ending at Bar 121.

106. Open a new Finder window by clicking on the Finder icon in the Dock.

107. Open Train Song – M Fein Mix.mp3 and compare this mixed version of the tune to your GarageBand mix.

108. Make any final adjustments to panning, volume, or effect plug-ins in your GarageBand file.

109. Drag the song-ending marker to Bar 121, as shown in Figure 15.48. If you don't do this, you will have lots of extra silence at the end of your file when you export the final mix.

Figure 15.48 Song-ending marker.

110.   Export the final mix by selecting Share > Export Song to Disk or Share > Send Song to iTunes.

111.   If you plan to burn this finished file to an audio CD, uncheck Compress in the Export window. This will export the final mix as a full CD-quality file. If you plan to post the file to a website or add it to your iPod, check Compress. A compressed file is great for the Internet or an iPod because it is significantly smaller (about 1/10th the size of a CD-quality file); however, you lose a small bit of quality. The most common compressed audio files are MP3 and AAC files.

Extensions

Download song stems from the Internet and remix hit songs. Many artists have started to post multitrack versions of their hit songs. The individual audio files are called *stems*. Nine Inch Nails currently has a website with multitrack versions of many of their songs and a forum to post your remix version (remix.nin.com). Radiohead has also posted multitrack versions of their songs "Nude" and "Reckoner." These files used to be available for purchase at Amazon.com and the iTunes Store; however, they are not currently available for purchase at the time of this publication. Try doing a Google search for "[name of artist] [name of song] stems" and see what you find!

16 Putting It All Together: Two Final Projects for Mixcraft or GarageBand

For the final practical activities chapter of this book, we have selected two projects that you can create using either Mixcraft or GarageBand:

- The Raven Retold, featuring the poetry of Edgar Allen Poe and an accompanying video.

- A chance to remix a song by Nine Inch Nails.

For these projects, we will give fewer specific steps and leave more space for creativity and experimentation. You are more on your own, which matches quite accurately the kinds of projects that you might encounter in the real world of digital audio production. Good luck! Refer to all the skills you have already learned, which will help you achieve impressive results with either of these final projects.

Lesson 1: The Raven Retold *by Richard McCready*

National Standards
2. Performing on instruments, alone and with others, a varied repertoire of music

3. Improvising melodies, variations, and accompaniments

4. Composing and arranging music within specified guidelines

6. Listening to, analyzing, and describing music

7. Evaluating music and music performances

8. Understanding relationships between music, the other arts, and disciplines outside the arts

9. Understanding music in relation to history and culture

Objectives
- Retell the story of Edgar Allan Poe's "The Raven."

- Rewrite the story and use it to accompany a video clip from a scary movie.

■ Record your own telling of the story, add music and effects, and export the final mix as a movie.

Class Time Required
You should be able to complete this lesson well in four one-hour sessions.

Materials
■ Mixcraft or GarageBand

■ Headphones or monitor speakers

■ Audio interface

■ Microphone

■ MIDI keyboard

■ Copy of Edgar Allan Poe's poem "The Raven"

■ Recording of "The Raven" by the Alan Parsons Project

■ Notepaper and pen or pencil

■ Video file from the companion DVD, entitled Video for The Raven.avi

Procedure
1. Read Edgar Allan Poe's poem "The Raven." You can find it in any collection of Poe's poems, which you can find in any library or online at www.houseofusher. net/raven.html. Find out about Poe's life and about the era in which he lived.

2. Listen to the recording of "The Raven" from the Alan Parsons Project's *Tales of Mystery and Imagination* album. You can download it from iTunes, or you can find it at YouTube.com by searching for "Alan Parsons Raven." Consider the differences between Poe's poem and the Alan Parsons Project's song. Both tell the same story and have the same intensity, yet the musical version tells the story in far fewer words. What do you think the point or the message of the story is? You might like to discuss the poem and the song with your music teacher or your English teacher.

3. Import the video file Video for The Raven.avi into Mixcraft or GarageBand. Watch the video and consider how dark and mysterious the setting of the video is. Can you see the connection between this video and "The Raven?" What similarities and commonalities can you find? In Poe's poem, the student responds to a sound from outside. It turns out to be a raven, whose presence affects him very deeply. In the movie, the young lady is dreaming heavily and responds to a sound, presumably from outside. At the end of the movie,

something frightens her. It is up to you to imagine what that is and how the two different media (the poem and the video) relate to each other.

4. Using notepaper and a pen or pencil, write out a script to retell the story of "The Raven" to go along with the video. You could write it as a solo recitation or involve some friends to make it into a play. Rehearse your script to make sure that it is shorter than the video. It is perfectly acceptable to have large passages of silence between the lines in your script—this helps to add tension. The presence of music in the final movie will ensure that silence in your script does not seem out of place.

5. Disable the video playback screen in the Sequencer program. Create an Audio track. Record and edit your script for "The Raven." Make sure you remember to use good recording techniques and check levels before beginning to read your script. Be prepared to do several takes and to record your script in small sections so you can edit later. Remember to strip the silence from the beginning and end of every recorded section and cross-fade any clips that overlap. Add compression, reverb, EQ, and other effects to your vocal recordings to make your voice sound spooky but still audible.

6. Re-enable the video screen and listen to your recorded script as you watch the video. Make changes to your recording if you need to. Make sure that your voice is clear and audible all the way through the video.

7. Add some Instrument tracks to the project. Record some spooky music using your MIDI keyboard (or Musical Typing). Use some of the virtual instruments or software instruments in the computer program and select the weirdest sounds you can find. Make your music frightening and unsettling. Use clusters of notes, unusual intervals, and strange chords. If you have a mod wheel and a pitch-bend wheel, use them! You will really have to let your imagination go crazy to make your composing/improvising effective in the movie. You want to get away from melody and predictability as much as possible.

8. If you play an acoustic instrument or an electric guitar, add an Audio track to the project and record some weird sounds from your instrument. Play your instrument in strange and different ways. (Just be sure not to break the instrument.) Try to make the instrument sound as different as possible from how one would expect it to sound. Add some effects to the track.

9. Mix your project. Add some panning to the sounds and automate them so they move between the left and right sides in the mix. This technique can make your listener very uncomfortable and even nauseated. It is a technique that you will hear often if you listen carefully to the soundtracks of professionally made horror movies. Add compression, EQ, reverb, and other effects to your individual tracks; add effects to the master mix fader if you want to apply

them to the whole mix. Make sure none of your volume faders goes into the red zone.

10.   Export your final project as a movie. Show it to your teachers and your friends. Look ahead to Chapter 17 for ideas on how to publish your movie online.

Extensions

Try to find the entire *Tales of Mystery and Imagination* album by the Alan Parsons Project and listen to the other songs. Read more of Edgar Allan Poe's poems and other works of fiction. Find some poems or stories that you can retell through music and video. Look at www.archive.org for some scary videos that you can download and use for your projects. Choose videos that are in .avi format. You can edit video on a PC using Mixcraft (editing video is the exact same method as editing audio) or on a Mac using iMovie. Publish your movies online for others to watch.

Lesson 2: Nine Inch Nails Remix *by Michael Fein*

National Standards

1. Singing, alone and with others, a varied repertoire of music

2. Performing on instruments, alone and with others, a varied repertoire of music

3. Improvising melodies, variations, and accompaniments

4. Composing and arranging music within specified guidelines

5. Reading and notating music

6. Listening to, analyzing, and describing music

7. Evaluating music and music performances

8. Understanding relationships between music, the other arts, and disciplines outside the arts

9. Understanding music in relation to history and culture

Objectives

■ Adjust the tempo and/or key of the song.

■ Remove audio regions from the song.

■ Import loops into the song.

■ Compose and record original musical ideas using the MIDI keyboard.

■ Compose and record original musical ideas using acoustic instruments or voice.

■ Add effect plug-ins to alter the sound of various tracks.

■ Use automation to mix the file.

■ Add photos or a video to the file.

■ Export the completed remix.

Class Time Required

You should be able to complete this lesson well in three one-hour sessions.

Materials

■ Remix entry at Wikipedia (en.wikipedia.org/wiki/Remix)

■ "The Hand That Feeds" by Nine Inch Nails from the album *With Teeth*

- The Hand that Feeds remix file (GarageBand or Raw format) available at remix.nin. com

- THTF Raw File Guide.pdf located on the companion DVD

Preparations

1. Read the Remix entry at Wikipedia (en.wikipedia.org/wiki/Remix) for background on remixing, its place in electronic and urban music, its influence on the other arts, and its connection with modern society.

2. Listen to the original version of "The Hand That Feeds" by Nine Inch Nails from the album *With Teeth*.

   - Download the file from the iTunes store, or

   - Listen to the song on YouTube by searching for "Hand That Feeds Nine Inch Nails."

3. Visit remix.nin.com and register at the site.

4. Listen to a variety of user-created remixes of "The Hand That Feeds" on the NIN remix site.

5. Click on the Listen link at the top of the site, as shown in Figure 16.1.

Figure 16.1 Click the Listen link.

a. Click on Search, type "The Hand That Feeds," and click the Search button, as shown in Figures 16.2 and 16.3.

Figure 16.2 Click Search.

Figure 16.3 Type "The Hand That Feeds" and click Search.

b. Click the Play button next to one of the remix files in the Results window, as shown in Figure 16.4.

Figure 16.4 Click the Play button to listen to one of the remix files.

6. Download the remix file from the NIN remix site.

a. Click the Mix link at the top of the site, as shown in Figure 16.5.

Figure 16.5 Click the Mix link.

b. Click the Download Multi-Tracks link, as shown in Figure 16.6.

Figure 16.6 Click the Download Multi-Tracks link.

c. Scroll down and locate The Hand That Feeds (see Figure 16.7). GarageBand users should download the GarageBand format file; Mixcraft users should download the Raw format file.

Figure 16.7 Download The Hand That Feeds files.

Your goal in this project is to create an original remix of the song that sounds quite different than the original NIN version of the song. The steps in the following section will serve as a guide, but you will need to experiment quite a bit to come up with something creative.

The only rule to remixing is that THERE ARE NO RULES!

Procedure

1. Open The Hand That Feeds remix file.

- GarageBand users: Simply copy The Hand That Feeds GarageBand file to your computer hard drive and open it.

- Mixcraft users: Your setup process is a bit more involved—sorry!

1. Create a new loop/beat-matched project.
2. Set the key of the song to A and the tempo to 128 bpm.
3. Import each Raw audio file.
4. Double-click one of the audio files. In the Sound tab, select Adjust to Project Tempo and set Detected Tempo to 128. Also select Adjust to Project Key and set Detected Key to A.

5. Repeat these steps with all of the Raw audio files.

6. Use THTF Raw File Guide.pdf to help assemble the loops.

2. Adjust the tempo and/or key of the song. The original song was recorded at 128 bpm in A minor.

- GarageBand users: Click on the Track Info pane and select Master Track. Adjust the tempo slider and/or select a new key.

- Mixcraft users: Double-click the green time window that displays the tempo/key and adjust as you wish. As long as you completed Step 1, the loops should tempo/key-stretch to the new project tempo/key.

3. Remove some audio regions. I suggest removing at least four tracks from the original. I typically remove the drums, percussion, and at least one very identifiable element of the song (for example, the guitar riffs). This will force you to replace those elements with something altogether different, drastically changing the sound of your remix.

4. Import a variety of loops. Drums and percussion loops are excellent choices, but you can also add pitched loops (such as electric piano, guitar, synths, bass, and so on) to the file.

5. Create new Software/Virtual Instrument tracks and use a MIDI keyboard to compose and record new musical ideas. I suggest using synth instruments to get an electronic sound or pads to add a layer of texture.

Tip: The A minor pentatonic scale (A-C-D-E-G) works great for this song (see Figure 16.8).

Figure 16.8 The A minor pentatonic scale.

---

6. Create new Audio tracks and record new musical ideas using acoustic instruments or your voice. Try recording electric or acoustic guitar, backing vocals, or even a wind instrument (saxophone, trumpet, and so on).

7. Add effects to the original Audio tracks and any additional tracks that you recorded. Don't be afraid of using fairly drastic effect plug-ins on the tracks or even adding effect plug-ins to the vocal tracks.

8. Modify the form of the song.

- Consider adding a breakdown section. In this sort of section, you would drop out all audio regions except for one or two and slowly build back up to the full instrumentation. For example, I could create a breakdown by dropping out all audio except for drums. After four bars, I could add in some bass and electric piano loops. After another four bars, I could improvise in A minor pentatonic on electric guitar. Finally, I could bring the rest of the audio material back in eight bars later.

- Copy and paste entire sections. GarageBand users can make use of the Arrange Track to help with this process. Simply Option-drag to copy an entire Arrange section.

- Remove entire sections. There is no law that says you need to include every part of the song when creating a remix.

9. Mix the file.

   a. Create a rough mix by setting the volume and panning of each track as you listen to the file. Be sure to make use of panning so some tracks are more to the left and others are more to the right.

   b. Add automation to the volume and panning to bring your mix to life. I suggest panning some tracks left to right and back and forth to get a really interesting panning effect. You can also use volume automation to fade tracks in and out or to simply make a track softer/louder in certain sections of the song.

10. Explore the Master Track.

   - GarageBand users: Add a mastering preset and adjust the settings of each effect as needed.

   - Mixcraft users: Use compressor, EQ, and reverb in the FX chain of the Master Track.

   - Fade into and/or out of the entire song.

11. Add photos or a video.

   - GarageBand users: Do a Google search for appropriate photos and compile them in the remix file.

   - Mixcraft users: Create a slideshow including pictures in PowerPoint and embed your exported remix to play through the presentation.

   - Search www.archives.org for video footage, save the file to your hard drive, and import the video. Consider modifying the tempo of the remix or adding/removing sections to fit the video. Consider compiling a variety of video clips together using iMovie or Windows Movie Maker and exporting them as a single video file. You may also use the video entitled "Video for The Raven" included on the companion DVD for "The Raven" project in this chapter.

12. Export your finished remix.

Extensions

Upload your finished mix to the NIN remix website.

1.   At the NIN remix site, click on Mix at the top of the site.

2.   Click Upload Remix and follow the onscreen instructions (see Figure 16.9).

Figure 16.9   Click Upload Remix.

Download and remix additional files from the NIN remix website or Real World Remixed (www.realworldremixed.com).

17 Putting It All Together

One of the most exciting aspects of making music with both Mixcraft and GarageBand is that both programs have the capability to create "ready-to-go" content that can be shared and distributed to a large audience instead of simply containing it within the educational space. Both teachers and students can quite easily take works that they have created with either program and upload them to a wide variety of accessible outlets, including stand-alone websites, blogs, wikis, podcasts, YouTube, or even commercial outlets, such as the iTunes Music Store. This last chapter of the book will examine the various ways you can accomplish this type of digital distribution and will touch on several related topics, such as copyright, licensing, paying royalties, and the remix/mashup culture. This chapter is intended to provide the next steps for the many different ways in which music educators can utilize both Mixcraft and GarageBand in the music classroom.

Getting the Music Off Your Computer

In each of the lessons contained in this book, you end up with some type of finished product—in most cases, a piece of music. When starting any of these lessons, teachers should ask always ask themselves, "What is my ultimate goal?" The easiest thing to do is to play the student work in the classroom for an opportunity for critique and reflection. But when this is finished, what happens to the music? The simplest thing to do is to have the students save their work to a removable storage device or burn their work to a CD. Burning files to an audio CD is quite simple with both Mixcraft and Garage-Band. (You can read the tutorial files on how to do this in both programs at the end of Chapters 2 and 3 and view the accompanying tutorial videos on the companion DVD.)

However, students in our classrooms today are more likely to consume their media in more non-physical formats, such as MP3 files. Many have been downloading, uploading, listening to, and sharing MP3 files for the past decade, using either somewhat nefarious peer-to-peer sharing networks (such as LimeWire or BitTorrent) or through legal outlets (such as iTunes, Pandora Radio, or Amazon). Rather than sticking with the first two, and perhaps more traditional, models of distribution (listening and burning), teachers might consider more current methods of digital distribution that the recording industry is slowly coming to accept as the future.

The easiest way to share student work (or teacher work, for that matter) with a large audience is by posting the work to a website and making the files available for listening, downloading, or both. In the past, creating a website that could accommodate such functionality required either some in-depth HTML programming skills or a relative or friend who knew how to program websites. Today, there are many templates and site-creation software programs and websites that allow you to do WYSIWYG (what you see is what you get) editing for the web. Apple users can utilize the iWeb application that comes with every Mac, and Windows users can utilize a wide variety of inexpensive web-authoring programs to do the same on a PC. These programs allow you to create some aesthetically pleasing sites with templated pages for uploading audio files as podcasts. The only potential downside to this method of website creation is that you will need some space on a web server, and you'll need some basic type of FTP software to transfer the website files you create to that server. Your school IT director should be able to help you with this.

A viable alternative to the software-based model of website creation is using site-authoring websites that are geared specifically toward education. The advantage of using these sites is that they are almost always free and easy to use. Although there are many choices out there, you should consider using Wikispaces (www.wikispaces.com), WordPress (www.wordpress.com), and EduBlogs (www.edublogs.com). These sites may not be specifically set up to share audio files, but they all have the functionality to do so. Teachers can create custom sites for their classes using any one of these suggestions, and they can post student work that can be shared with a global audience. It is truly up to the teacher to decide the purpose of the site. Some possibilities include:

- A blog where student work is posted so that others can comment on it, or a class-specific website that acts as the homepage for a student-run record label that includes recordings students have created as well as recordings of school ensembles.

- A website that acts as an electronic "refrigerator" for friends and family to see and/ or hear student projects.

- A site where teachers share lesson plans and examples of student work with other educators.

Web 2.0 resources (sites that allow for true two-way interaction between author and user) are wonderful ways to share work with others. However, in some school districts they do not allow teachers to use third-party sites such as these to post student work. Instead, some prefer teachers to use the proprietary templated sites that are available with the server platform that the school adopts. It is recommended that teachers check with their IT departments to see what the district policy is for this option.

For the purposes of this text, the following tutorial helps to illustrate the process of uploading an audio file to Wikispaces. This process is extremely similar on almost every other site-creation website.

Posting Audio Files to a Website

When your students have finished working on their projects (which could be almost any of the projects included in this text), the first step in sharing the projects with a global audience is getting them off of the student computer and onto yours. Easy ways to accomplish include the following:

- Have students email you their work as an attachment.

- Use a removable flash drive (also known as a *jump drive* or *thumb drive*) to save the students' work from their computers onto the drive, and then load the projects onto your computer.

- Have students save their work to a network-based folder to which you have access. (Many schools have teacher drop boxes where students can submit their work.)

- Have students burn their work to a CD-R or CD-RW so that you can load it onto your machine for downloading. Although this is certainly the most time-consuming of the methods discussed, it may sometimes be necessary to do this if the student work is very large in size (for example, video or film projects).

When the students' work is on your computer, the next step is to create a website using one of the many education-focused web-hosting sites available (if the district policy allows you to do so). In this example, we will select Wikispaces (www.wikispaces.com) to illustrate the process.

Step 1: Registering for a Wikispaces Account

Wikispaces is a website that provides teachers with free space to create educational environments for their students. The term *wiki* means that the site has functionality that can allow students to edit any of the content on the site. For the purposes of this exercise, we are simply using the free space that Wikispaces provides as a place to post student work. Teachers can opt out of the wiki functionality and use the site as a way to post student work only (though there is a Discussion Board feature that can facilitate critique and reflection on student work).

The first step in getting student work on the Wikispaces site is to create an account. As an educator, you are entitled to create a free account for use with your students. Once you have clicked the appropriate options on the Wikispaces homepage, you will be prompted to create an account. Complete the form (see Figure 17.1) and click Join.

After you have registered for an account, you'll need to select a name for your site, choose the level of permissions (Protected or Private is recommended for use with students), and select the type of wiki you are creating (K-12 Education). When you have completed these steps, you are ready to start creating your site.

Create Your Free K-12 Wiki

Username	example
Password	••••••
Email Address	example@example.com

We will not spam or share your email address.

Make a Wiki? ◉Yes ○No
Create a wiki now or after you join.

Wiki Name example

Choose a name between 3 and 32 characters long.

Wiki Permissions ○ Public (free)
　　　　　　　　Everyone can view and edit your pages.
　　　　　　　○ Protected (free)
　　　　　　　　Everyone can view pages, only wiki members can edit them.
　　　　　　　◉ Private (**free for educators** otherwise $5/month)
　　　　　　　　Only wiki members can view and edit pages.

Educational Use ☑ I certify this wiki will be used for K-12 education.
　　　　　　　　We may contact you via email to verify use.

Join

Figure 17.1   Wikispaces account signup window.

Step 2: Creating Your Website

When you first enter your new site, it should look something like what you see in Figure 17.2.

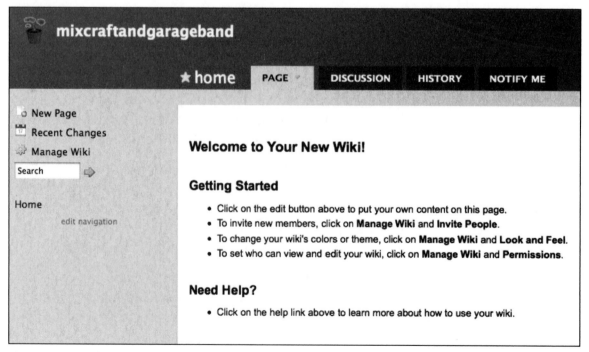

Figure 17.2   Wikispaces new website.

To start creating the page, you'll need to click the Edit button. This will allow you to edit the page much as you would a Microsoft Word document. You will notice a toolbar pop up when you are in Edit mode (see Figure 17.3). Along with the familiar word processing controls, you'll see a File option in the center of the toolbar. This is the option you'll need to select for inserting/uploading audio files to your site. Click on the File button, and you will be prompted to select the type of file you want to upload (see Figure 17.4). Select Audio File to upload an audio file or Video File to upload a video.

Figure 17.3 Wikispaces Edit toolbar.

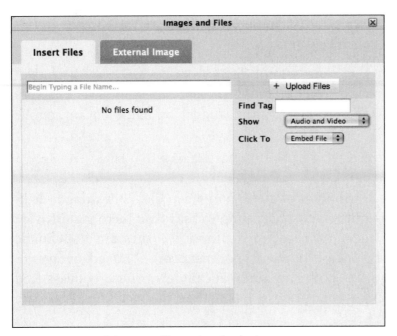

Figure 17.4 Wikispaces file upload window.

You'll need to select the student work that you would like to upload from your computer to the site, wait for the file to upload, and then double-click on the file name from the Images and Files menu (refer to Figure 17.4). Most similar websites have the same file-uploading process.

When your audio file is uploaded, it will be placed into the edited page as an Audio Player file with whatever audio format the work is in (.mp3, .mov, .aiff, .wav, .wmv) displayed. You can type text above it to identify the file. When you click Save, you'll see what the page will look like when viewed by others. You should see an audio player appear (see Figure 17.5) on your page. Users then simply click the Play button to hear the student work.

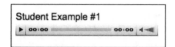

Figure 17.5 Wikispaces audio player.

From a pedagogical standpoint, you can utilize Wikispaces (or any other similar type of website) to upload all of your student work for others to listen to and comment on. You can easily send out the URL of the site to students, parents, administrators, and colleagues to share what your students have accomplished in your class with Mixcraft and GarageBand. In addition to audio files, you can post videos, podcasts, images, and text on these types of websites. One benefit to utilizing these sites is that they are free and easy to use. Another is that you don't need to pay to store these files on their servers. Lastly, by utilizing these types of sites, you're giving your students a real-life experience in the digital distribution model of the music business. You can spur many conversations by posting their files online, including copyright (discussed later in this chapter), music piracy, and digital citizenship.

Once again, be sure to consult with your school district's policy on posting student work online, specifically with regard to maintaining student anonymity. It may very well be against your district's policy to identify the student by name on any public website.

Creating Your Own Podcast Channel

Another method for the digital distribution of audio and video files is creating a dedicated podcast channel. There are quite a few podcasting websites out there that provide educators with free space for student work. Two of those websites are PodOmatic (www.podomatic.com) and MyPodcast (www.mypodcast.com). The advantage to using sites such as these is that they both can automatically generate a podcast feed URL, which is necessary to include your podcast channel on the biggest podcast site of them all, iTunes.

The following tutorial will take you through the process of setting up a podcast channel using PodOmatic.

Step 1: Creating a PodOmatic Account

The first step in creating your own podcast channel is registering for an account at any of the many podcast-hosting sites available. PodOmatic has a self-explanatory registration process that requires you to input some basic personal information, including an email address (see Figure 17.6). You will want to choose the Basic option to avoid paying any fees. After you enter your basic information, you will be required to enter the desired URL for your podcast site. You might want to use your school's name in the URL or a music-oriented name to help your students (and their parents) find your site.

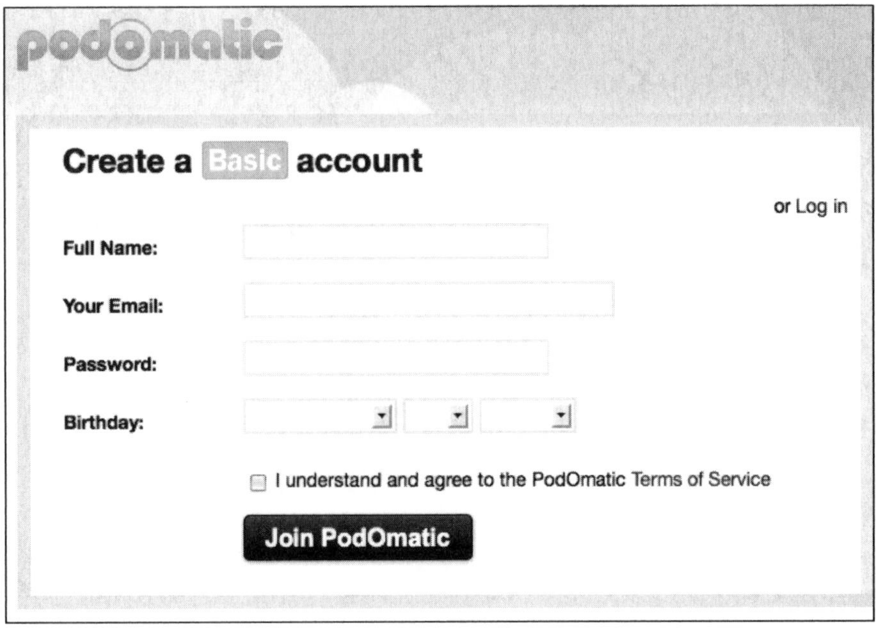

Figure 17.6   PodOmatic account registration.

After you go through the initial registration process, a confirmation email will be sent to your email address. When you get this email, you'll be ready to start editing your podcast channel.

The single most important part of your podcast site is the Podcast RSS Feed URL (which will be listed in the center of the My Podcast administration page of your account). The URL will look something like this: http://mixcraftandgarageband.podomatic.com/rss2.xml. The reason why this URL is so important is that in order to get your podcasts on the iTunes Music Store, you need to submit this address. Any other podcast-hosting site that you choose should have this important address available.

Posting podcasts on PodOmatic is a very similar process to creating a webpage on Wikispaces. You will need to locate the Post an Episode feature on the My Podcast administration page, upload student work, and enter pertinent information about the content. You can use your PodOmatic site either as the main way for your students to access their work or as a space to host the files that are then accessed through iTunes. The advantage to putting the podcasts on iTunes is that it is a wildly popular way of distributing and downloading podcasts, and it once again gives your students a real-world experience. Creating an iTunes Music Store podcast site is free and easy.

Step 2: Getting Your Podcasts on iTunes

The first step in creating your iTunes Music Store podcast channel is creating an iTunes account. (If you purchase music through iTunes, you already have one of these.) After you have created your account, you will need to locate the Podcast section of the iTunes

Figure 17.7 iTunes Music Store Podcast Quick Links menu.

Music Store. Once there, you will need to click Submit a Podcast in the Podcast Quick Links menu (see Figure 17.7).

After you click on the Submit a Podcast link, you will come to a page that asks you for your podcast feed URL (see Figure 17.8). All you need to do is copy the RSS feed URL from your PodOmatic My Podcast administration page, paste it into the window, and click Continue. After you do so, you'll have to complete a few forms that ask questions about the purpose and content of your podcast channel, and you will need to name your podcast channel. After 24 to 48 hours, your podcast channel should appear on the iTunes Music Store. When it is up, you can send your students, parents, administrators, and colleagues there to download the students' work.

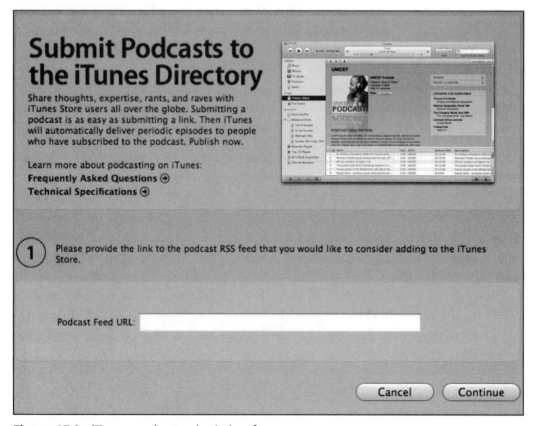

Figure 17.8 iTunes podcast submission form.

It should be noted that any audio and video file can be a podcast, so if you're looking to get your students' work to a wide audience, this might be a good option for you. Teachers should be cautious about what they post to the iTunes Music Store (as it is a premier site for music and video distribution), so we recommend that anything posted be carefully screened first by the teacher. From a copyright perspective, students should avoid using copyright-protected materials in their podcasts—and if they do, they should keep the use within Fair Use guidelines (which will be discussed a bit later in this chapter).

From a pedagogical standpoint, having student work posted on the iTunes Music Store is a wonderful opportunity to provide students with a real-world experience. Creating work in Mixcraft and GarageBand provides them with many opportunities to create professional-sounding (and professional-looking) results, and sharing their work with a global audience is exciting for anyone.

Posting Work to YouTube

If your students' work in Mixcraft and GarageBand includes film and video scoring, you might consider posting their finished works on YouTube—the most popular video sharing and viewing site on the Internet. Although there are alternatives to YouTube, such as TeacherTube and SchoolTube, none is quite the same as the original. Creating an account on YouTube is very easy, and it allows you to also create your own YouTube channel, which can serve as the central hub for sharing student video files.

The first step in creating your own YouTube channel for use with your students is creating a YouTube account. Simply click on Create Account in the upper-right corner of the YouTube homepage to do so. The form you'll need to complete includes your email address and username. Use your school email address and make your username something to do with your school (examplevillehsmusic, for example). When you have completed the form and accepted the YouTube Terms and Conditions, you'll need to confirm your email address. Next, log into your YouTube account and start uploading!

To upload a video to YouTube, you will need to click on the Upload button at the top of the YouTube toolbar (see Figure 17.9). You can customize the look and feel of your channel if you wish (you might consider adding your school mascot as the channel icon) and set permissions for commenting, viewing, embedding, and sharing.

Figure 17.9 YouTube toolbar.

YouTube allows you to post videos up to 15 minutes in length and 2 GB in size, and there is no limit to the number of videos you can upload to your channel. Things to consider when deciding whether to utilize YouTube include:

■ Does your school block YouTube?

- Does your school district allow student work to be posted on YouTube?

- Does the content of the video include copyright-protected material? If so, does it fall within the Fair Use guidelines?

When uploading a video, you will be asked to title, describe, categorize, and tag the movie and to set the privacy settings. For maximum privacy, you can set any video to Unlisted or Private and send an email or the URL to your students so that they can view it. Otherwise, it will automatically be set to Public, where anyone can view the work.

The pedagogical rationale for having your students utilize a 21st-century tool to upload the work they have created in Mixcraft and GarageBand may not always be enough for your district to allow you to post student work to YouTube. However, the benefits include giving your students a real-world experience in content sharing and distribution, as well as giving them an opportunity to share their work with a large audience.

Distributing Student Work Commercially

The final, and perhaps most exciting, way to distribute student work (or any recordings that you make of your performing ensembles with Mixcraft and GarageBand) is to make them commercially available through sites such as the iTunes Music Store, Amazon, and Rhapsody. Before considering this option, you will need to check with your administration about creating a bank account specifically for your music department, which may be required to sell content through this type of channel.

There are quite a few ways to get your students' work (and your own) available for commercial release. The easiest way is to use a website that specializes in digital content distribution. Two such sites are TuneCore (www.tunecore.com) and Catapult (www.catapultdistribution.com). Both sites allow you to upload content to outlets such as the iTunes Music Store, Amazon, and Rhapsody for a nominal annual fee ($20 to $25). In addition to these fees, you are required to pay any associated mechanical licensing fees for recordings of copyright-protected works through sites such as Harry Fox (www.harryfox.com). By far the best option is to distribute only original work to get the most money in return. (Mechanical licensing fees can be up to 20 cents per song after paying additional processing fees.)

This model of distribution can offer some very exciting opportunities for your music program.

- You can record and edit your concerts with Mixcraft and GarageBand and sell them through outlets such as the iTunes Music Store, Amazon, and Rhapsody. After paying the associated royalties, you can use the remaining income as a fundraiser for your music department.

- Your students can create and run their own record label (there are many examples of this already in place in high schools across the U.S.), giving them valuable real-world experience in the music industry.

- As a musician yourself, you might want to consider selling your original music through this outlet.

The pedagogical rationale for exploring the commercial digital distribution model includes giving your students not only real-world experience in the music industry, but also business experience. A student-run record label has many cross-curricular dimensions and could easily be a part of the business department of your school as well. Additionally, making recordings of your performing ensembles available through this medium is a terrific opportunity for fundraising.

Copyright Issues and Fair Use

When creating and sharing anything in the digital environment, you will no doubt run across copyright issues pretty quickly. There are several excellent texts and websites available on this subject, but the following should give you some idea of what you can and cannot do in relation to working with Mixcraft and GarageBand and your students. One tremendous advantage that both programs have is that they include very large selections of copyright- and royalty-free loops for students to use without any fear of violating copyright law. In fact, you can hear many of the loops included in both programs in commercially released music, TV shows, and commercials. Because both programs also allow you to record and import copyright-protected material, teachers and students should be aware of some basic rules.

- If you make recordings of copyright-protected works, you need to pay the mandatory mechanical licensing fees if you want to make more than one copy, regardless of whether you charge people for them.

- If you include copyright-protected recordings in your work, you should not use more than 10 percent or 30 seconds of the original work. As long as your use is educational, it will be considered a fair use of the work. However, if you plan on making the work commercially available, you will need to either get permission or pay the required royalties (sometimes both) to do so.

- If your students create their own original works, they should seriously consider getting their work registered for copyright protection. They can do this by visiting www.copyright.gov and paying the $35 per work fee. (A work can be an entire album.)

Many students today enjoy making what are known as *remixes* and *mashups*. A remix can be defined as a rethinking of a work by editing the recording and adding new material to it. A mashup can be defined as mixing two different songs together to form a new work. There are numerous examples of both genres available on the Internet.

Both Mixcraft and GarageBand are perfectly suited to allow students to make remixes and mashups, and it may be something that you decide to explore with them. In terms of copyright, as long as your use of others' work is noncommercial and purely educational (along with the 10 percent, 30-second rule), you can make remixes and mashups with your students. If you decide to post their work in any of the methods described earlier in this chapter, you may be told to remove the work (in what is known as a *takedown notice*) from your site. If you do receive one of these requests, you must remove the content in question immediately to avoid potential prosecution. A good rule of thumb is to always try to post original work only and avoid posting anything that contains copyright-protected materials.

Fair use allows educators to utilize copyright-protected materials in ways that non-educators cannot. There are four factors in determining whether your use of a work is fair. They include:

- **Purpose.** Is your purpose for using the work educational?

- **Nature.** What was the nature of the original work? Was it commercially available?

- **Amount.** How much of the work are you using?

- **Effect.** What effect will this have on the commercial viability of the work?

Fair use can be somewhat confusing. Educators should refer to fairuse.stanford.edu for a clear understanding of what may and may not be considered a fair use of copyright-protected material.

Another possibility in terms of teaching your students about copyright and licensing is to explore the Creative Commons (CC) licenses. These alternative licenses allow for much broader use of materials. Teachers should strongly consider showing their students the Creative Commons site (www.creativecommons.org) and discussing the issues surrounding copyright protection and the alternative licensing ideas that Creative Commons offers.

Final Thoughts

Mixcraft and GarageBand provide educators and students with tremendously powerful tools for student creativity. As we head further into the 21st century, music educators must find ways of including the entire school population in the music program. Connecting with the other 80 percent of the students who are not currently involved with the performance aspect of school music programs affords exciting opportunities for both students and teachers to explore the creative energy that is inside each of us. Mixcraft and GarageBand allow nontraditional music students (as well as traditional music students) to explore music creation without having to know how to read or notate music. There are countless examples of well-known musicians (including some of the best songwriters ever to walk the planet) making beautiful music without knowing all of the mechanics of music.

Incorporating composition, podcasting, film scoring, and all of the other exciting learning opportunities that Mixcraft and GarageBand afford students into a school music program is one of the few ways to truly incorporate 21st-century learning skills into a school environment. Both programs are inexpensive and easy to use and help foster creativity. Can you think of any good reason *not* to start using these programs in your school today?

It is the sincere hope of the authors of this text that we have provided you, the educator, with a clear set of strategies, basic knowledge of the software programs, and lesson ideas for incorporating Mixcraft and GarageBand into your music curriculum.

Appendix A: Existing Resources

Acoustica, the manufacturers of Mixcraft, make a book entitled *Mixcraft for the Classroom*. For details on this book, contact SoundTree at 800-963-8733.

Acoustica also has produced some tutorial videos on learning Mixcraft. Visit www.youtube.com and search for the word "Mixcraft" or visit the official tutorial video site at www.youtube.com/user/acoustica222.

There's also a support page on the main Acoustica website with links to download a PDF manual and more. See www.acoustica.com/mixcraft/support.htm.

Apple, the makers of GarageBand, have produced a number of tutorials on how to use GarageBand. You can view these at www.apple.com/ilife/tutorials/#garageband.

Apple also has a 122-page PDF file on using GarageBand '09, which you can download from manuals.info.apple.com/en_US/GarageBand_09_Getting_Started.pdf.

Finally, there are various official training books and videos. See www.peachpit.com and www.macprovideo.com/browse/GarageBand for more details.

Appendix B: Setting Up Your Computers and Suggested Equipment You May Need

To work with students on any music software, it is best to have access to more than one computer if at all possible. A lab of computers is optimal. This can include a lab being used by other subjects, not just music.

You can work with one machine at a Smart Board or with an LCD projector and screen, but it will be impossible for students to work at their own pace if each student is not sitting at his or her own station.

Collaborative projects can obviously work well, but once again, having more than two or three students sitting at a station is difficult.

You can obviously share the files/songs generated by students using Mixcraft or GarageBand, and it is wise to carefully choose where the files/songs are being stored so that you can share them easily across a school network or by means of a thumb drive or a hard drive.

Mixcraft and GarageBand both require a fairly decent computer in terms of age, processor speed, and RAM. The operating system you are running (especially for GarageBand on a Mac) is critical.

Mixcraft is now at version 5. If you already have an earlier version, an update is recommended. This will cost perhaps $17 per computer, depending on how many copies you already have. A computer running XP, Vista, or Windows 7 is required, with 2 GB of RAM and at least a 1-GHz processor. More RAM and a faster processor are always recommended.

Note that there is a free limited-time download of Mixcraft that allows you to try the full functionality of the program for a specified period of time. Eventually, though, you will need to purchase Mixcraft. The prices for education are very reasonable. Consult www.soundtree.com for details, especially for multi-seat pricing (more than five copies), where prices are either $27 or $34 per copy.

GarageBand is part of the suite called iLife '09 or iLife '11, and the required specifications for your Mac are detailed at www.apple.com/ilife/systemrequirements.html. Note that Leopard (10.5.6) or a newer operating system is required. You may be able to use these curriculum resources with an earlier version of GarageBand, but iLife '09 or iLife '11 is recommended as of this writing. iLife '11 contains some useful new features for GarageBand, which are detailed on the Apple website. That said, GarageBand '09 is also perfectly fine to use for the purposes of this book.

Several other pieces of equipment are useful to have, although you can complete some of this curriculum with nothing more than a computer and the software.

Audio Interface and Microphones

If you're going to record sound straight onto your computer using either Mixcraft or GarageBand, an audio interface is highly recommended. You will never get decent results by using the internal microphone on your computer and nothing else. Nor will you get great results by connecting a low-cost consumer-style microphone straight into the 1/8-inch connector on the side or back of your computer.

All professional recordings of any quality utilize an audio interface, which is a small box (connected to your computer via USB, typically) that converts sound waves into a digital signal. You connect a microphone or a guitar into the audio interface. This becomes your whole playback and recording system for your computer. Entry-level audio interfaces start at just under $100 each and include devices such as the M-Audio Fast Track II and the Alesis iO2. There are quite a few to choose from—consult www.soundtree.com for details.

Microphones

Together with an audio interface, you'll want to have some microphones on hand to use. There's a wide range of choices of microphones and wide price disparity and quality, but most people are fine starting with a low-cost dynamic microphone for around $60 per microphone. Shure, AKG, and Audio-Technica, for example, all have entry-level dynamic microphones. For more advice, consult www.soundtree.com. These kinds of microphones come with a cable called an *XLR cable* (with three pins on the end of it). Your audio interface will have that port on it.

Some people prefer to use a USB microphone as an alternative to an audio interface. This is a microphone with a USB connection on the end of it, and it performs the same task as an audio interface; so you can avoid buying an audio interface and a microphone, and instead just get a USB microphone. The downside to this approach is that you cannot connect an electric or acoustic electric guitar, because there is no 1/4-inch input port on a USB microphone. You can only use it for recording voice or capturing the signal of an acoustic instrument.

MIDI Keyboards

Both Mixcraft and GarageBand allow you to enter notes by clicking them onto the screen or by means of a virtual onscreen keyboard that appears for musical typing. You may, however, wish to use a "real" physical keyboard with the software. There are several types of keyboards available. All you really need for these software programs is a silent keyboard (sometimes known as a *controller* or a *mother keyboard*). This is a keyboard without its own sounds—just a set of keys. It will most likely connect to your computer via USB (like the audio interface). Keyboards like these come in a variety of sizes and prices. They start at $49 for a Korg nanoKEY and go up to $99 or so for an M-Audio or Alesis MIDI keyboard—and then all the way to more sophisticated controllers with extra knobs and controls built into them. Once again, consult www.soundtree.com for details.

Some teachers will already have a keyboard in their classroom—perhaps even one with sounds—but they may never have tried to connect it to their computer. If this applies to you, take a look on the back of the keyboard. Does it have a USB port? If so, it can connect to your computer via USB. If it has an older-style MIDI port on it, you will need a USB-to-MIDI cable to connect it. These cables typically cost $39 or so.

If you are connecting a keyboard with its own sounds, you can probably turn the volume setting down on the keyboard itself. The software will generate the sounds you hear once you start playing music.

Guitars

Both software titles are fantastic for recording and playing back real guitar. You'll most likely need a guitar with an audio output (that is, the means to connect a 1/4-inch TS or instrument cable into the guitar and then into an audio interface). You won't get decent results without an audio interface. You can use either a full-on solid-body electric guitar or a semi-acoustic guitar. Both software programs give you virtual amplifier combinations that you dial up to get a distorted or effected sound (see Chapters 8 and 9 for more details), so you don't actually need a guitar amplifier—just the guitar. If all you have is an acoustic guitar with nowhere on it to connect a cable, then you can mike up the guitar using a microphone, the same as you would do if you were recording vocals. You'll need a decent microphone stand in this scenario.

Lab Control Systems and Speakers or Headphones

You'll definitely need to find a way to listen to student work, and it will be pretty much essential for students to work without their neighbors hearing them, or else noisy chaos will envelop your lab! For that reason, the very least you need is a set of headphones for each student, so they can plug these into their computers (or the output ports of their audio interfaces—recommended) and work without distracting anyone else. Decent headphones start at around $29 per pair. You can also get headphone splitters to allow two students to connect to the same port on one computer.

There's absolutely no need to have a set of speakers at each computer, and they can in fact cause feedback trouble when you are recording. You will, however, want at least one decent set of speakers at the teacher station, which you can use for playing back student work.

If you get a Lab Control System such as the Korg GEC (Group Education Controller), you get the added benefits of being able to listen in at any student station and being able to talk one on one with students without leaving your desk. This allows each computer to be connected to your teacher station using an audio network. You can team up students sitting at different stations all over your room, and they can converse without having to leave their stations. In this scenario, everyone is wearing headsets (like airline pilots or call-center employees) that have a microphone and headphones combined. You can also easily play a student's work by routing the output of the student's computer straight through to your teacher speakers whenever you like. And you can easily play music or talk to all of the students at once without having to take off your headset, thus saving your precious vocal cords from wear and tear!

Desktop Microphone Stands

This is a useful peripheral item to have if you're planning to record podcasts, vocals, or voiceovers. These start at around $13 each and are a much better alternative to holding a microphone in your hand, as this causes unwanted noise and may cause the signal level to go up and down if you don't hold the microphone at a solid distance from the sound source. If you're using a USB microphone, these often come with their own desktop microphone stands. You may also use a regular floor-based microphone stand, but they are quite bulky when you are in a computer lab with lots of students.

Drivers and Latency

One final issue to consider, especially when you connect a keyboard or a guitar to your computer, is the issue of latency (literally, lateness), which is a delay between playing something into your computer and hearing your signal coming back from the computer. This can be a common problem, and it occurs rather more on Windows PCs than on Macs. If you experience latency when using a MIDI keyboard or guitar, there are ways to mitigate this. The best way to lower your latency is by ensuring you have enough RAM on your computer. Having an audio interface connected will often lower your latency as well.

With Mixcraft, you may wish to download an ASIO driver for your computer from www.asio4all.com. This will actually improve the performance of your computer's soundcard—and the ASIO driver is free. There are other technical ways you can reduce latency on Windows or Mac, too. As ever, talk to experts such as SoundTree for some advice.

If you buy an audio interface or a MIDI keyboard, you may need to load a driver. (This assists your computer in detecting the device when you plug it in.) Some devices don't need a driver (the technical phrase for these devices is that they are *class-compliant*), and drivers are sometimes more needed for Windows PCs than for Macs. As ever, if your computer is not detecting the presence of your keyboard or audio interface, call someone for assistance!

Troubleshooting

The first place to look for help is usually your computer's internal settings. Most issues with music software relate to your computer failing to "see" or detect the devices you are connecting (typically, the MIDI keyboard or audio interface).

In Windows, go to Control Panel > Sounds and Audio Devices and ensure that you have the correct settings for your input and playback device. On a Mac, you can do this by clicking on the Apple icon at the very top left of your screen and then choosing System Preferences > Sound.

Both Mixcraft and GarageBand also have settings that you should check when you first run the software. We looked at these in Chapters 2 and 3.

Appendix C: Mixcraft Shortcuts

T his appendix contains some useful Mixcraft shortcuts. Ctrl refers to the Control key—use the key at the bottom left of your computer's keyboard.

Ctrl+A	Select All
Ctrl+Shift+A	Select all regions on a selected track
Ctrl+B	Burn a project (render a stereo mix)
Ctrl+C	Copy a selected region
Ctrl+D	Move the selected track down in the list of tracks
Ctrl+E	Add a new Virtual Instrument (MIDI) track
Ctrl+F	Freeze a selected track (so it cannot be edited)
Ctrl+G	Add a new Audio track
Ctrl+H	Add (import) a new sound file
Ctrl+I	Trim silence from a selected region (remove gaps)
Ctrl+J	Join selected regions together (remove space between)
Ctrl+K	Normalize the volume of selected region(s)
Ctrl+L	Solo a selected track
Ctrl+M	Mute a selected track
Ctrl+N	Start a new project
Ctrl+O	Open a project
Ctrl+P	Print (when Score view is displayed)
Ctrl+Alt+P	Open Preferences
Ctrl+R	Start recording in Mixcraft
Ctrl+S	Save a project
Ctrl+T	Split a region (where the cursor is positioned)
Ctrl+U	Move the selected track up in the list of tracks
Ctrl+V	Paste (if you have copied something using Ctrl+C)
Ctrl+W	Merge two or more regions to a new clip
Ctrl+X	Cut a selected region

Ctrl+Y	Redo the last action (if you have undone it)
Ctrl+Z	Undo the last action
+	Zoom in on the project
—	Zoom out on the project
0 (above QWERTY keys)	Fit the project in one screen
Alt+1	Fade in a selected region at fast speed
Alt+2	Fade out a selected region at slow speed
Alt+3	Fade in a selected region at medium speed
Alt+4	Fade out a selected region at medium speed
Alt+5	Fade in a selected region at slow speed
Alt+6	Fade out a selected region at fast speed
Alt + drag region	Make a copy of a region
Double-click on track	Select all regions
Double-click on region	Open the Sound Edit screen
Mouse scroll wheel	Zoom in/out horizontally on the project (like using the + and — keys)

Appendix D: GarageBand Shortcuts

This appendix contains some useful GarageBand shortcuts. Command refers to the key just to the left of the spacebar on your computer, which may also be marked with the icon ⌘ or may have an Apple icon.

Opt refers to the Option key (just to the left of the Command key). This may also be marked as Alt. Control refers to the key to the left of the Option key, which may also be marked Ctrl.

Command+A	Select all
Command+Shift+A	Show/hide Arrange Track
Command+B	Show/hide Master Track
Command+Shift+B	Show/hide Podcast track
Command+Opt+B	Show/Hide Movie track
Command+C	Copy a selected region or a selection of notes/events
Command+D	Create a duplicate track (based on the kind of track that is selected)
Command+E	Show/hide Editor (at the bottom of the screen) for audio or MIDI data
Command+F	Display chord in the main display at the bottom of the screen
Command+Shift+F	Display absolute time in the main display at the bottom of the screen
Command+Opt+F	Display bars/beats in the main display at the bottom of the screen
Command+Control+F	Display key/tempo/signature in the main display at the bottom of the screen
Command+G	Snap to Grid (and you then need to choose your grid value)
Command+Shift+G	Show/hide the alignment guide in the timeline as you drag a region
Command+H	Hide GarageBand
Command+I	Show/hide the Track Info screen (on the right)
Command+J	Join selected regions (to make one larger region)
Command+K	Show/hide the virtual onscreen MIDI keyboard

Command+Shift+K	Show/hide the Musical Typing keyboard
Command+L	Show/hide the Loop Browser
Command+M	Minimize GarageBand (keep it running but stop displaying it)
Command+N	Start a new project
Command+Shift+N	Add new Basic track (an Audio track with no effects)
Command+Opt+N	Add an extra track (you can choose what type of track)
Command+O	Open an existing GarageBand project/file/song
P	Add a marker (only works with movie or podcast projects)
Command+P	Print (when Score view is displayed)
Command+Shift+P	Page Setup (when working with a score)
Command+Q	Quit GarageBand
Command+R	Show/hide the Media Browser
Command+Shift+R	Activate/deactivate ducking (auto-reduction of volume levels)
Command+S	Save your project
Command+Shift+S	Save As (give a project a new title)
Command+T	Split a region (where the cursor is positioned over a selected region)
Command+U	Activate/deactivate the metronome
Command+Shift+U	Activate/deactivate the count-in bar
Command+V	Paste (if you have copied something using Command+C)
Command+W	Close a song in GarageBand, but keep the software running
Command+X	Cut a selected region
Command+Z	Undo the last action performed
Command+Shift+Z	Redo the last action (if you have just clicked to undo an action)
Command+,	Open Preferences
Alt + drag region	Make a copy of a region
Double-click on a track	Select all regions
Double-click on a region	Open Edit screen (at bottom)

Index

License Agreement/Notice of Limited Warranty

By opening the sealed disc container in this book, you agree to the following terms and conditions. If, upon reading the following license agreement and notice of limited warranty, you cannot agree to the terms and conditions set forth, return the unused book with unopened disc to the place where you purchased it for a refund.

License

The enclosed software is copyrighted by the copyright holder(s) indicated on the software disc. You are licensed to copy the software onto a single computer for use by a single user and to a backup disc. You may not reproduce, make copies, or distribute copies or rent or lease the software in whole or in part, except with written permission of the copyright holder(s). You may transfer the enclosed disc only together with this license, and only if you destroy all other copies of the software and the transferee agrees to the terms of the license. You may not decompile, reverse assemble, or reverse engineer the software.

Notice of Limited Warranty

The enclosed disc is warranted by Course Technology to be free of physical defects in materials and workmanship for a period of sixty (60) days from end user's purchase of the book/disc combination. During the sixty-day term of the limited warranty, Course Technology will provide a replacement disc upon the return of a defective disc.

Limited Liability

THE SOLE REMEDY FOR BREACH OF THIS LIMITED WARRANTY SHALL CONSIST ENTIRELY OF REPLACEMENT OF THE DEFECTIVE DISC. IN NO EVENT SHALL COURSE TECHNOLOGY OR THE AUTHOR BE LIABLE FOR ANY OTHER DAMAGES, INCLUDING LOSS OR CORRUPTION OF DATA, CHANGES IN THE FUNCTIONAL CHARACTERISTICS OF THE HARDWARE OR OPERATING SYSTEM, DELETERIOUS INTERACTION WITH OTHER SOFTWARE, OR ANY OTHER SPECIAL, INCIDENTAL, OR CONSEQUENTIAL DAMAGES THAT MAY ARISE, EVEN IF COURSE TECHNOLOGY AND/OR THE AUTHOR HAS PREVIOUSLY BEEN NOTIFIED THAT THE POSSIBILITY OF SUCH DAMAGES EXISTS.

Disclaimer of Warranties

COURSE TECHNOLOGY AND THE AUTHOR SPECIFICALLY DISCLAIM ANY AND ALL OTHER WARRANTIES, EITHER EXPRESS OR IMPLIED, INCLUDING WARRANTIES OF MERCHANTABILITY, SUITABILITY TO A PARTICULAR TASK OR PURPOSE, OR FREEDOM FROM ERRORS. SOME STATES DO NOT ALLOW FOR EXCLUSION OF IMPLIED WARRANTIES OR LIMITATION OF INCIDENTAL OR CONSEQUENTIAL DAMAGES, SO THESE LIMITATIONS MIGHT NOT APPLY TO YOU.

Other

This Agreement is governed by the laws of the State of Massachusetts without regard to choice of law principles. The United Convention of Contracts for the International Sale of Goods is specifically disclaimed. This Agreement constitutes the entire agreement between you and Course Technology regarding use of the software.